# Building Capacity to Reduce BULLYING

## Workshop Summary

Patti Simon and Steve Olson, *Rapporteurs*

Board on Children, Youth, and Families

Committee on Law and Justice

INSTITUTE OF MEDICINE AND
NATIONAL RESEARCH COUNCIL

THE NATIONAL ACADEMIES PRESS
Washington, D.C.
**www.nap.edu**

THE NATIONAL ACADEMIES PRESS   500 Fifth Street, NW   Washington, DC 20001

NOTICE: The workshop that is the subject of this workshop summary was approved by the Governing Board of the National Research Council, whose members are drawn from the councils of the National Academy of Sciences, the National Academy of Engineering, and the Institute of Medicine.

This activity was supported by Contract No. HHSH250200976014I/HHS25034018T between the National Academy of Sciences and the Health Resources and Services Administration of the U.S. Department of Health and Human Services. The views presented in this publication do not necessarily reflect the views of the organizations or agencies that provided support for the activity.

International Standard Book Number-13:   978-0-309-30398-9
International Standard Book Number-10:   0-309-30398-2

Additional copies of this workshop summary are available for sale from the National Academies Press, 500 Fifth Street, NW, Keck 360, Washington, DC 20001; (800) 624-6242 or (202) 334-3313; http://www.nap.edu.

For more information about the Institute of Medicine, visit the IOM home page at: www.iom.edu.

Copyright 2014 by the National Academy of Sciences. All rights reserved.

Printed in the United States of America

Suggested citation: IOM (Institute of Medicine) and NRC (National Research Council). 2014. *Building capacity to reduce bullying: Workshop summary.* Washington, DC: The National Academies Press.

# THE NATIONAL ACADEMIES
*Advisers to the Nation on Science, Engineering, and Medicine*

The **National Academy of Sciences** is a private, nonprofit, self-perpetuating society of distinguished scholars engaged in scientific and engineering research, dedicated to the furtherance of science and technology and to their use for the general welfare. Upon the authority of the charter granted to it by the Congress in 1863, the Academy has a mandate that requires it to advise the federal government on scientific and technical matters. Dr. Ralph J. Cicerone is president of the National Academy of Sciences.

The **National Academy of Engineering** was established in 1964, under the charter of the National Academy of Sciences, as a parallel organization of outstanding engineers. It is autonomous in its administration and in the selection of its members, sharing with the National Academy of Sciences the responsibility for advising the federal government. The National Academy of Engineering also sponsors engineering programs aimed at meeting national needs, encourages education and research, and recognizes the superior achievements of engineers. Dr. C. D. Mote, Jr., is president of the National Academy of Engineering.

The **Institute of Medicine** was established in 1970 by the National Academy of Sciences to secure the services of eminent members of appropriate professions in the examination of policy matters pertaining to the health of the public. The Institute acts under the responsibility given to the National Academy of Sciences by its congressional charter to be an adviser to the federal government and, upon its own initiative, to identify issues of medical care, research, and education. Dr. Victor J. Dzau is president of the Institute of Medicine.

The **National Research Council** was organized by the National Academy of Sciences in 1916 to associate the broad community of science and technology with the Academy's purposes of furthering knowledge and advising the federal government. Functioning in accordance with general policies determined by the Academy, the Council has become the principal operating agency of both the National Academy of Sciences and the National Academy of Engineering in providing services to the government, the public, and the scientific and engineering communities. The Council is administered jointly by both Academies and the Institute of Medicine. Dr. Ralph J. Cicerone and Dr. C. D. Mote, Jr., are chair and vice chair, respectively, of the National Research Council.

**www.national-academies.org**

## PLANNING COMMITTEE ON INCREASING CAPACITY FOR REDUCING BULLYING AND ITS IMPACT ON THE LIFECOURSE OF YOUTH INVOLVED[1]

**FREDERICK P. RIVARA** (*Chair*), Seattle Children's Guild Endowed Chair in Pediatrics, Professor of Pediatrics, University of Washington School of Medicine

**CATHERINE BRADSHAW,** Professor, Associate Dean for Research and Faculty Development, Curry School of Education, University of Virginia

**NINA FREDLAND,** Associate Professor, Texas Woman's University College of Nursing

**DENISE GOTTFREDSON,** Professor at the University of Maryland Department of Criminal Justice and Criminology

**NANCY GUERRA,** Professor of Psychology, Associate Provost for International Programs and Director, Institute for Global Studies, University of Delaware

**MEGAN A. MORENO,** Associate Professor of Pediatrics, University of Washington

**JONATHAN TODRES,** Professor of Law, Georgia State University College of Law

*Project Staff*

**PATTI SIMON,** Project Director
**TARA MAINERO,** Research Associate
**STACEY SMIT,** Senior Program Assistant

*Board on Children, Youth, and Families Staff*

**KIMBER BOGARD,** Director
**FAYE HILLMAN,** Financial Associate

*Committee on Law and Justice Staff*

**ARLENE LEE,** Director

---

[1] Institute of Medicine planning committees are solely responsible for organizing the workshop, identifying topics, and choosing speakers. The responsibility for the published workshop summary rests with the workshop rapporteurs and the institution.

# Reviewers

This workshop summary has been reviewed in draft form by individuals chosen for their diverse perspectives and technical expertise, in accordance with procedures approved by the National Research Council's Report Review Committee. The purpose of this independent review is to provide candid and critical comments that will assist the institution in making its published workshop summary as sound as possible and to ensure that the workshop summary meets institutional standards for objectivity, evidence, and responsiveness to the study charge. The review comments and draft manuscript remain confidential to protect the integrity of the process. We wish to thank the following individuals for their review of this workshop summary:

**David V. B. Britt,** Retired CEO, Sesame Workshop
**Deborah Gross,** Johns Hopkins University School of Nursing and Medicine
**Mark L. Hatzenbuehler,** Columbia University
**Tracy Vaillancourt,** University of Ottawa

Although the reviewers listed above have provided many constructive comments and suggestions, they did not see the final draft of the workshop summary before its release. The review of this workshop summary was overseen by **Hugh H. Tilson,** University of North Carolina Gillings School of Global Public Health. Appointed by the National Research Council and the Institute of Medicine, he was responsible for making certain that an independent examination of this workshop summary was carried out in accordance with institutional procedures and that all review comments were carefully considered. Responsibility for the final content of this workshop summary rests entirely with the rapporteurs and the institution.

# Contents

1 Introduction and Overview — 1

## PART I
## UNDERSTANDING BULLYING

2 Overview of Bullying and Victimization — 9
3 Targets of Bullying and Bullying Behavior — 19

## PART II
## CONTEXTS FOR PREVENTION AND INTERVENTION

4 School-Based Interventions — 35
5 Family-Focused Interventions — 49
6 Technology-Based Interventions — 57
7 Community-Based Interventions — 65
8 Peer-Led and Peer-Focused Programs — 73
9 Laws and Public Policies — 81

## PART III
## FUTURE DIRECTIONS AND OVERALL THEMES

10 Translating Bullying Research into Policy and Practice — 91
11 Reflections of School Personnel and Student Perspectives — 103
12 Final Thoughts — 113

## APPENDIXES

| | | |
|---|---|---|
| A | References | 121 |
| B | Workshop Agenda | 131 |
| C | Workshop Statement of Task | 139 |

# 1

# Introduction and Overview[1]

Bullying—long tolerated as just a part of growing up—finally has been recognized as a substantial and preventable health problem. Bullying is associated with anxiety, depression, poor school performance, and future delinquent behavior among its targets, and reports regularly surface of youth who have committed suicide at least in part because of intolerable bullying. Bullying can also have harmful effects on children who bully, on bystanders, on school climates, and on society at large. Bullying can occur at all ages, from before elementary school to after high school. It can take the form of physical violence, verbal attacks, social isolation, spreading rumors, or cyberbullying.

Increased concern about bullying has led 49 states and the District of Columbia to enact anti-bullying legislation since 1999. In addition, research on the causes, consequences, and prevention of bullying has expanded greatly in recent decades. However, major gaps still exist in the understanding of bullying and of interventions that can prevent or mitigate the effects of bullying.

On April 9–10, 2014, the Board on Children, Youth, and Families of the Institute of Medicine (IOM) and the National Research Council (NRC)

---

[1] The planning committee's role was limited to planning the workshop, and the workshop summary has been prepared by the workshop rapporteurs as a factual summary of what occurred at the workshop. Statements, recommendations, and opinions expressed are those of individual presenters and participants, and are not necessarily endorsed or verified by the Institute of Medicine or the National Research Council, and they should not be construed as reflecting any group consensus.

held a 2-day workshop titled "Building Capacity to Reduce Bullying and Its Impact on Youth Across the Lifecourse." The purpose of this workshop was to bring together representatives of key sectors involved in bullying prevention to identify the conceptual models and interventions that have proven effective in decreasing bullying, to examine models that could increase protective factors and mitigate the negative effects of bullying, and to explore the appropriate roles of different groups in preventing bullying.

At the workshop more than 20 presenters reviewed research on bullying prevention and intervention efforts as well as efforts in related areas of research and practice, implemented in a range of contexts and settings, including

- Schools
- Peers
- Families
- Communities
- Laws and Public Policies
- Technology

Following the research presentations, two panels of discussants—one consisting of youth and one of school personnel—provided additional perspectives to the workshop. Box 1-1 lists the workshop's objectives. An additional 200 people registered for the webcast of the workshop and contributed questions to the discussion sessions.

The planning committee for the workshop consisted of Frederick P. Rivara (chair), Seattle Children's Guild Endowed Chair in Pediatrics and professor of pediatrics at the University of Washington School of Medicine; Catherine Bradshaw, professor and associate dean for research and faculty development at the University of Virginia Curry School of Education; Nina Fredland, associate professor at the Texas Woman's University College of Nursing; Denise Gottfredson, professor in the Department of Criminal Justice and Criminology at the University of Maryland; Nancy Guerra, professor of psychology, associate provost for international programs, and director of the Institute for Global Studies at the University of Delaware; Megan Moreno, associate professor of pediatrics at the University of Washington; and Jonathan Todres, professor of law at the Georgia State University College of Law.

The workshop was funded by the Health Resources and Services Administration (HRSA) of the U.S. Department of Health and Human Services. The website for the workshop is http://www.iom.edu/activities/children/reducingbullying/2014-apr-01.aspx.

## BOX 1-1
## Workshop Objectives[a]

The overall objective of the workshop was to highlight current research on bullying prevention. More specifically, workshop presentations and discussions addressed the following questions:

- What are the underlying knowledge base and conceptual models that guide the design, delivery, and evaluation of bullying prevention and intervention efforts?
- Are there specific interventions that are effective in decreasing bullying and the antecedents to bullying?
- What programs designed to address other negative adolescent behaviors (e.g., substance abuse or delinquency) are also effective at preventing or reducing bullying?
- Are there specific models and interventions that increase protective factors and mitigate the negative health impacts of bullying?
- What are the key sectors involved in bullying prevention and intervention? How does involvement or lack of involvement by key sectors influence opportunities and barriers to implementing a blueprint for bullying prevention and intervention? What are some appropriate roles for each of the key sectors in preventing bullying?

---

[a] The workshop statement of task is included in Appendix C.

## COMMENTS FROM THE SPONSOR

"When it comes to bullying prevention, we know we can still do a lot better," said Michael Lu, associate administrator for maternal and child health at HRSA, during his opening remarks at the workshop. According to the Centers for Disease Control and Prevention's 2011 Youth Risk Behavior Surveillance System, 20 percent of high school students in the United States experience bullying (Eaton et al., 2012), Lu said. The School Crime Supplement, based on statistics from the National Center for Education and the Bureau of Justice, indicated that, in 2009, 28 percent of students in grades 6 through 12 experienced bullying (Robers et al., 2012). Many millions of children are bullied each year, Lu said.

In 2004 HRSA launched the first federal anti-bullying campaign, including the first federal website to prevent bullying. Today, these efforts have evolved into a collaborative interagency initiative hosted at http://www.stopbullying.gov, which is a one-stop shop for all federal bullying prevention resources. "We have made great strides in raising public awareness about bullying and its negative impact on youth," Lu said. But "there are still way too many children and youth in this country who are being bullied every day."

A major obstacle to improvement is the amount that remains unknown, Lu observed. That knowledge gap was the motivation behind HRSA's interest in sponsoring an IOM/NRC workshop to highlight current research on bullying prevention. The workshop was designed to consider what does and does not work and to derive lessons learned. "Five years from now, or 10 years from now, as a nation, we will know a lot better about how to prevent bullying and reduce its impact on millions of children, youth, and families across the lifecourse," Lu said.

"This is an extraordinary gathering," he concluded. "We have policy makers, researchers, educators, practitioners, and the public with us today in the room or online. We all come from different parts of the country. We come from different backgrounds, different walks of life. . . . [But] we have all gathered here today for one common purpose, united by one common cause—to reduce bullying and its impact on youth."

## ORGANIZATION OF THE WORKSHOP SUMMARY

The organization of the workshop summary follows the organization of the workshop panels and presentations. As noted earlier, this organization highlights the contexts in which bullying prevention interventions occur and the sectors that are engaged in these efforts. The contents of this summary reflect the research presented at the workshop and the discussions that followed but should not be perceived as a comprehensive review of bullying prevention research. Specific topics (e.g., cyberbullying) and populations (e.g., lesbian, gay, bisexual, and transgender [LGBT] youth, racial/ethnic minority youth) are considered within the broader contexts framework. This was a deliberate decision on the part of the planning committee, explained Bradshaw. For example, in putting together the workshop agenda, the planning committee considered having a separate panel that focused on issues of diversity (e.g., ethnic or cultural diversity, individuals with disabilities, LGBT populations) and bullying prevention, she said. Given the heterogeneity of these groups and their experiences, the planning committee decided instead to include issues and research related to diversity "as a thread" throughout the workshop, said Bradshaw. This decision should not be perceived as omission or lack of emphasis on issues of diversity, and discussions of these topics can be found in this summary in presentations by Susan Limber, the Dan Olweus Distinguished Professor at the Institute on Family and Neighborhood Life at Clemson University (see Chapter 2); Jaana Juvonen, professor in the Developmental Psychology Program at the University of California, Los Angeles, and Dorothy Espelage,

Edward William Gutgsell and Jane Marr Gutgsell Endowed Professor in the Department of Educational Psychology at the University of Illinois, Urbana-Champaign (see Chapter 3); and Mark Hatzenbuehler, assistant professor of sociomedical sciences at Columbia University's Mailman School of Public Health (see Chapter 9).

Similarly, while the workshop includes two reaction panels—one of school personnel and one of students—to offer their perspectives on the workshop presentations, these should not be viewed as the only stakeholder perspectives that would enhance an overall discussion of bullying prevention. The planning committee's decision not to include additional stakeholder reaction panels—of parents and caregivers, for example—should not be viewed as an omission, but rather as a function of what was considered to be feasible within the format of a 2-day workshop. Discussions of additional stakeholder groups can be found in this summary in presentations by Melissa Holt, an assistant professor at the Boston University School of Education (see Chapter 5); Deborah Gorman-Smith, professor in the School of Social Service Administration at the University of Chicago (see Chapter 5); Asha Goldweber, a behavioral health researcher in SRI International's Center for Education and Human Services (see Chapter 7); and Joseph Wright, professor and vice chair in the Department of Pediatrics and professor of emergency medicine and health policy at The George Washington University Schools of Medicine and Public Health (see Chapter 7).

The summary is organized into 3 parts and 12 chapters. Part I, which includes Chapters 2 and 3, describes a basis for understanding bullying. Part II, which includes Chapters 4 through 9, examines the contexts for prevention and intervention. Part III, which includes Chapters 10 through 12, describes possible future directions and overall themes that were discussed at the workshop. Each of the chapters is described briefly below.

Following this introduction, Chapter 2 provides an overview of bullying and victimization, including definitions, prevalence, and consequences. Chapter 3 reviews what is known about the targets of bullying and bullying behavior, including recent research on the neurobiological impact of bullying. Chapter 4 takes a closer look at school-based interventions, including characteristics of effective school interventions, the influence of school climate, and school policies to address bullying. Chapter 5 considers family-focused interventions and the role of parents and caregivers in bullying prevention. Chapter 6 focuses on technology-based interventions and includes a discussion of cyberbullying. Chapter 7 considers community-based interventions, including the role of health care professionals in bullying prevention. Chapter 8 reviews the research on peer-led and peer-focused interventions, which includes a discussion of both positive and negative peer influence. Chapter 9 provides an overview of laws and policies related to bullying and what is known about their effectiveness. Chapter 10 considers how to translate research on bullying prevention to policy and practice. Chapter 11 includes highlights from two reaction panels—one composed of school personnel and one of students—who offered their perspectives on the workshop presentations. Finally, Chapter 12 includes highlights from the workshop sessions and areas for future research as identified by individual members of the workshop planning committee.

# Part I

# Understanding Bullying

# 2

# Overview of Bullying and Victimization

---

**Key Points Made by the Speaker**

- A recently developed uniform definition of bullying will help researchers assess the scope and effects of bullying. (Limber)
- Although prevalence rates vary with the timeframe examined, the measurement approach used, the informant, and the geographic location of the study, 20 to 30 percent of children report having been bullied at least once in the past year, and more than 10 percent of children report having been bullied two to three or more times per month in the past 2 months. (Limber)
- Bullying can have harmful effects not only on the targets of bullying but also on children who engage in bullying behaviors, on bystanders, on school climates, and on society at large. (Limber)
- The continued collection of data on bullying will help to indicate whether prevention efforts are helping to change bullying rates. (Limber)

---

Concerns about bullying have grown dramatically in recent years, noted Susan Limber, the Dan Olweus Distinguished Professor at the Institute on Family and Neighborhood Life at Clemson University, in her introductory overview of bullying and victimization, but what exactly is "bullying"? Without a consistent definition of bullying, it becomes more difficult to understand the scope and magnitude of the problem, to measure the impact of bullying on children, and to prevent bullying.

After concerns about inconsistent definitions were raised at the first Federal Partners in Bullying Prevention Summit, which took place in 2010, the Centers for Disease Control and Prevention and the U.S. Department of Education launched an initiative to develop a uniform definition of bullying. With input from a panel of researchers and practitioners, the following definition was established (Gladden et al., 2014, p. 7):

> Bullying is any unwanted aggressive behavior(s) by another youth or group of youths . . . that involves an observed or perceived power imbalance and is repeated multiple times or is highly likely to be repeated. Bullying may inflict harm or distress on the targeted youth including physical, psychological, social, or educational harm.

The first key element of this definition, Limber said, is that bullying involves unwanted aggressive behavior—the targeted youth wants the aggression to stop. Bullying does not include playful taunting or teasing, although it can be a challenge for adults and other youth to tell whether behaviors are unwanted or not. The definition also describes aggression as the intentional use of harmful behaviors that are threatened or actual. The focus, Limber explained, is on whether the aggressor intends to use harmful behaviors, not on whether the aggressor intends the target to experience an injury.

The second key element in the definition, Limber said, is that bullying involves an imbalance of power. The aggressor is using observed or perceived personal or situational characteristics to exert control over the target or to limit his or her ability to respond or stop the aggression. Power differences can be characterized by many factors, including physical characteristics such as differences in size, age, or strength, but they can also include such factors as popularity or demographic characteristics, including whether or not a child is a member of a majority or a minority racial or ethnic group. Power differences can also include distinctions in social, academic, or other skills or abilities; access to resources; the ability to reach an entire student body with messages or images sent online; and the power of numbers, Limber said.

A third key element of bullying, she said, is its repetitive quality. Children who are targets of bullying often experience multiple incidents or a pattern of aggressive behavior against them. According to the definition, a single incident can be considered bullying if there is a strong likelihood that it will be followed by more like it. However, even though bullying typically is repeated over time, a one-time occurrence can be bullying, and adults should not wait for a pattern to emerge before responding, Limber said.

The uniform definition also acknowledges that bullying often inflicts harm or distress on the targeted youth, although this is not a requirement for a behavior to qualify as bullying, Limber noted. Not all bullied youth may be able to immediately identify or express what harm or distress they may have experienced from bullying, she said. For example, a child with developmental delays or disabilities may not always recognize that he or she is being harmed by being taunted or teased, but may be bullied nonetheless, Limber said.

## THE CHARACTERISTICS OF BULLYING

The uniform definition document recognizes two distinct modes of bullying, Limber explained. The first is *direct bullying*, which occurs in the presence of a targeted youth. The second is *indirect bullying*, such as the spreading of a rumor or encouraging others to exclude a peer.

The uniform definition also enumerates distinct types of bullying. For example, *physical bullying* includes such acts as hitting, kicking, punching, spitting, tripping, and pushing. *Verbal bullying* can include taunting, name-calling, sexual comments, or threatening words, notes, or gestures. *Relational bullying* is designed to harm reputations and relationships through, for example, social isolation, spreading rumors, or posting embarrassing images.

The terms "violence" and "bullying" are sometimes used interchangeably, and bullying is clearly a form of aggressive behavior, Limber said. But while all bullying is aggression, not all aggression is bullying, she observed. For example, a fight or a nasty argument between two peers of equal power or strength certainly is aggressive behavior but probably would not be characterized as bullying.

The World Health Organization has defined *violence* as "the intentional use of physical force or physical power, threatened or actual, against another person or against a group or community" (Dahlberg and Krug, 2002 p. 5). Thus, it overlaps with bullying but is not synonymous with bullying (see Figure 2-1). Some bullying may constitute discriminatory harassment under federal law. In a "Dear colleague" letter issued in 2010, the U.S. Department of Education's Office for Civil Rights clarified the relationship between bullying and discriminatory harassment and reminded schools of their obligations under anti-discrimination statutes (U.S. Department of Education, 2010). The letter notes that bullying of an individual based on race, color, national origin, sex, or disability can be a civil rights violation if it is "sufficiently serious that it creates a hostile environment

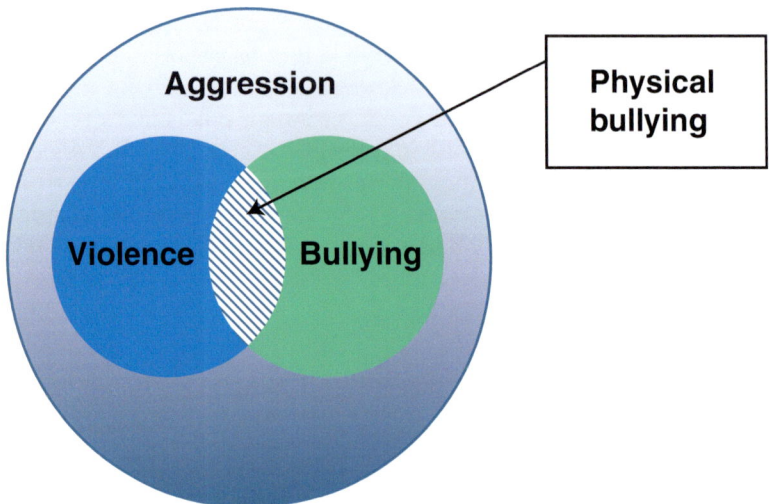

**FIGURE 2-1** Physical bullying is a subset of both aggression and the narrower category of violence.
SOURCE: Limber presentation, 2014.

and such harassment is encouraged, tolerated, not adequately addressed, or ignored by school employees."

## THE PREVALENCE OF BULLYING

In a review of more than 90 studies that had examined bullying prevalence among children and youth, Cook et al. (2010a) found that the prevalence rates vary according to the timeframe examined, the measurement approached used, the informant, and the geographic location of the study. Were children asked how much bullying they had experienced in the past year, the past 6 months, or the past week? Was bullying defined, and if so, how was it defined? Was the information derived from self-reports, peer reports, or teacher reports? Was bullying being examined in the United States or other countries?

For data on prevalence, Limber cited four national surveys that focus on slightly different age groups. The School Crime Supplement to the National Crime Victimization Survey (NCVS) found that 28 percent of 12- to 18-year-olds said they had been bullied at school in 2011 (Robers et al., 2012). The Youth Risk Behavior Survey (YRBS), which focuses on high school students, reported that in 2011, 20 percent of students had been bullied on school property during the previous year (Eaton et al., 2012).

The Health Behavior in School-Aged Children (HBSC), which collects data from a nationally representative sample of children and youth in grades 5 through 10, reported that during the 2009–2010 school year, 28 percent of youth had been bullied at school at least once in the previous 2 months, while 11 percent of youth had been bullied two to three times per month or more during this timeframe (Iannotti, 2014). The National Survey of Children's Exposure to Violence, which involved a national telephone survey of caregivers and youth with an age focus from 2 to 17, found that 13 percent of children had been physically bullied and 20 percent had been teased or emotionally bullied during the previous year (Finkelhor et al., 2009).

Researchers interested in examining the prevalence, nature, and effects of bullying often have analyzed the experiences of three distinct groups of children directly involved in bullying, Limber said. The first group consists of youth who bully others but are not themselves bullied. The literature refers to these youth as aggressors, perpetrators, or bullies. The second group consists of youth who are bullied but do not bully others. Sometimes they are referred to as targets or victims. The third group consists of youth who both are bullied themselves and also bully other youth. They often are referred to in the literature as bully–victims.

Cook et al. (2010a) found that children who are bullied constitute the largest proportion of students involved in bullying, followed by youth who bully, and finally youth who are bullied and also bully others. One study of third through twelfth graders who were involved in bullying two to three times per month or more, found these three categories to account for 13 percent (children who are bullied), 4 percent (children who bully others), and 3 percent (children who are bullied and also bully others) of all students in these grades (Limber et al., 2013).

According to data from the HBSC, students in grades 5 through 10 who are bullied two to three times per month or more at school most often experience verbal bullying and the spreading of lies (see Figure 2-2). Similarly, the NCVS found that verbal bullying and rumor spreading were the most common forms of bullying for sixth through twelfth graders (see Figure 2-3).

According to Cook et al. (2010a), boys and girls experience relatively similar rates of being bullied. On the other hand, Limber said, this meta-analysis found that boys were almost twice as likely as girls to bully others and were about 2.5 times as likely to both bully others and be bullied. The prevalence of different types of bullying also differs between boys and girls. According to the NCVS, girls are more likely than boys to indicate that they have been bullied through name-calling, rumor spreading, social exclusion, and cyberbullying, while boys are more likely than girls to say that they have been physically bullied (Eaton et al., 2012).

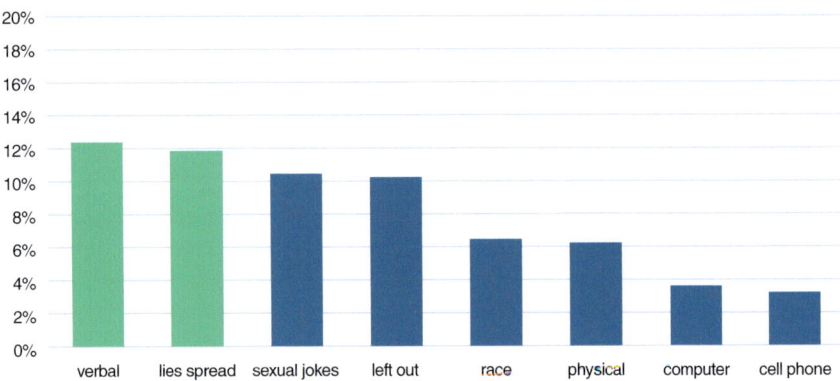

**FIGURE 2-2** Prevalence of different types of bullying.
NOTE: The types of bullying that occurred most often are highlighted in green.
SOURCE: Limber presentation, 2014. Data from HBSC, 2013.

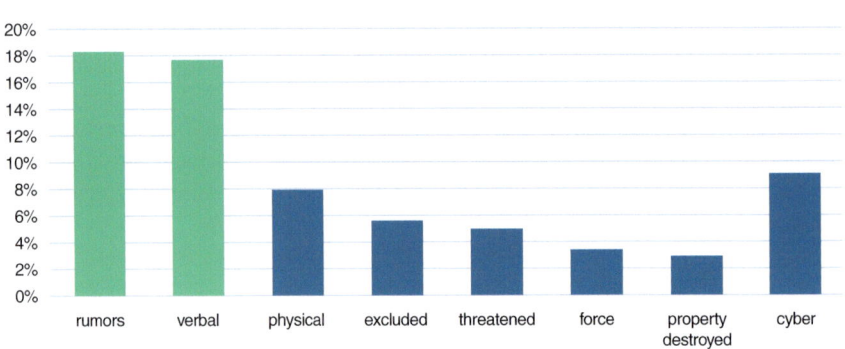

**FIGURE 2-3** Students ages 12 through 18 who are bullied during the school year most often experience rumors and verbal bullying.
NOTE: The types of bullying that occurred most often are highlighted in green.
SOURCE: Limber presentation, 2014. Data from Robers et al., 2013.

Children's experiences with bullying also vary according to their age, Limber said. The likelihood of being bullied is greatest in elementary and middle school and decreases throughout the high school grades (see Figure 2-4). Similarly, Limber et al. (2013), in a survey of more than 20,000 students in grades 3 through 12, found that rates of being bullied were highest among third graders and thereafter decreased steadily through elementary, middle, and high school both for boys and for girls.

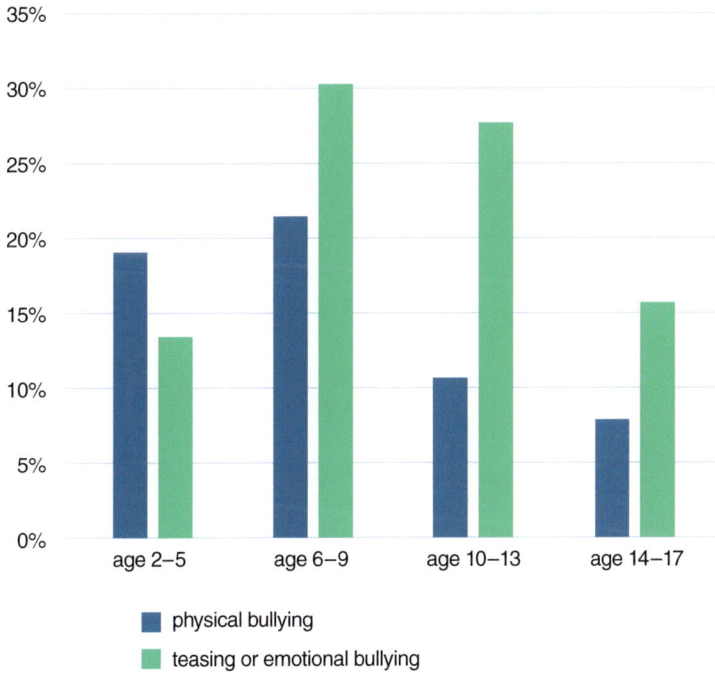

**FIGURE 2-4** The likelihood of being bullied is greatest in elementary grades and decreases through middle and high school.
SOURCE: Limber presentation, 2014. Data from Finkelhor et al., 2009.

Although bullying victimization is particularly likely in middle childhood, the specific forms of bullying that children are most likely to experience vary by age, depending on the children's verbal, cognitive, and social development and on circumstances, Limber said. For example, rates of cyberbullying rise from middle school to high school and peak in about the tenth grade (Robers et al., 2013).

Somewhat different age patterns are observed for self-reports of bullying others and of being a bully–victim, Limber said. In a large-scale survey of students in grades 3 through 12, Limber et al. (2013) found that among boys, bullying others increased steadily from about grade 3 through around grade 12, but among girls, rates of bullying others peaked in eighth grade (see Figure 2-5). However, Cook et al. (2010a) found that rates of bullying others decreased from age 3 through age 18 while the likelihood of being a bully–victim peaked in the adolescent years before then decreasing.

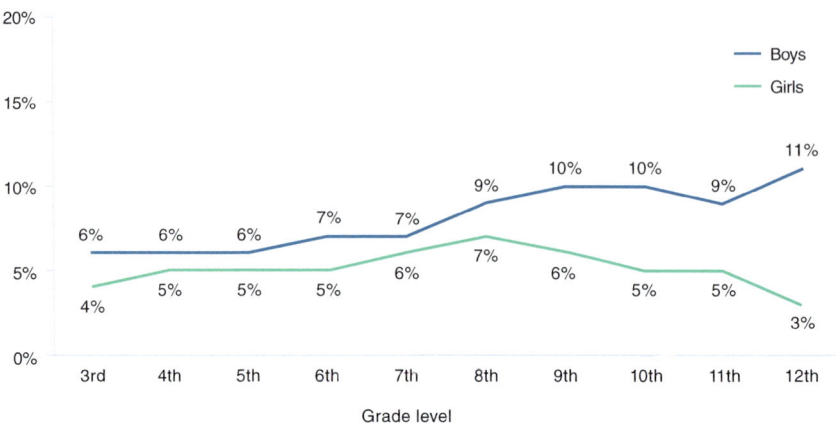

**FIGURE 2-5** The percentage of third through twelfth graders who have bullied other students two to three times per month or more rises until eighth grade for boys and girls and continues to rise after that for girls.
SOURCE: Limber et al., 2013.

## CHANGES OVER TIME

Despite increased attention to bullying since the early 2000s, the extent to which the rates of bullying have changed over time remains unclear, Limber said. Time trends depend on the data source, the gender of the participants, and the frequency of involvement, she added.

The percentage of students who said they were bullied occasionally—defined as once or more in the past couple of months—decreased between 2001/2002 and 2005/2006 by 16 percent for boys and 15 percent for girls, according to data from the HBSC (Molcho et al., 2009). Frequent victimization decreased by 5 percent for boys and 6 percent for girls during this time period. Data from the NCVS showed that the percentage of 12- to 18-year-olds who said they were bullied at school decreased by about 12 percent between 2007 and 2011, but the trend was much more pronounced for boys than girls (Robers et al., 2010, 2012, 2013). Data from the YRBS, which looks at high school students' experiences in the previous year, showed no changes between 2009 and 2011, which are the only 2 years for which data are comparable, given changes in the wording of questions over time (Eaton et al., 2009, 2012).

These data need to continue to be gathered and analyzed, Limber emphasized, because they will help to indicate whether bullying prevention efforts are changing the rates of bullying.

## THE CONSEQUENCES OF BULLYING

The consequences of bullying include not only the effects on the targets of bullying but also long-term outcomes for children who engage in bullying behavior, effects on bystanders, effects of bullying on the broader school climate, and the costs of bullying to society, Limber said.

Limber added that a very large body of research points to an association between being bullied and later internalizing problems and that a number of recent longitudinal studies have confirmed that being bullied is associated with the later development of a variety of issues: internalizing problems, including depression, anxiety, agoraphobia, panic disorder, and low self-esteem (Copeland et al., 2013; Faris and Felmlee, 2011; Ttofi et al., 2011a); psychosomatic problems, including headaches, stomach pain, sleeping problems, and poor appetite (Gini and Pozzoli, 2013); and school avoidance and lower academic achievement (Buhs et al., 2006, 2010). Some researchers have also found that peer victimization is associated with later externalizing behaviors, such as such as aggression, delinquency, and misconduct (Reijintjes et al., 2010).

Although researchers have concluded that there is a relationship between bullying and suicide-related behaviors (Hertz et al., 2013), relatively few longitudinal studies have been conducted to explore the causal links between bullying and later suicidal ideation, attempts, or deaths by suicide. Researchers have found that being bullied in childhood predicted later suicide attempts and deaths by suicide for girls but not for boys, after controlling for prior depression and conduct problems (Klomek et al., 2013), and that boys identified as bully–victims were at increased risk of suicidal thoughts and attempts in young adulthood (Copeland et al., 2013). However, this connection should not be overstated or misinterpreted, Limber said. The causes of suicide are complex, and many individual, relational, community, and societal factors can contribute to the risk of suicide (CDC, 2012). When researchers used data from the National Violent Death Reporting System to look at the precipitating circumstances for youth ages 10 through 17 who had died by suicide, they found that school-related problems were a precipitating circumstance in about one-quarter of the deaths (Karch et al., 2013). A small percentage of these—12 percent—appear to be related to bullying, Limber said. To put that number in context, she added, intimate-partner relationship problems were identified as a precipitating circumstance in about one-half of the deaths.

Longitudinal research of children who engage in bullying behavior also points to reason for concern, Limber said. For example, research has found that boys who bullied peers in middle school were four times as likely as peers to have three or more criminal convictions as young adults (Olweus, 1993), and boys who frequently bullied others were at high risk for later criminality when accompanied by a high level of psychiatric symptoms (Sourander et al., 2007). A meta-analysis of 18 studies found that bullying others was related to a greater likelihood of being involved in later criminal behavior and antisocial behavior (Ttofi et al., 2011b). In addition, Espelage et al. (2012) found that bullying others was associated with later sexual harassment of others among middle school students.

By one estimate, more than 80 percent of bullying is witnessed by others (O'Connell et al., 1999), and research suggests that bullying can have significant effects on bystanders (Polanin et al., 2012). Bystanders report feeling anxiety and insecurity (Rigby and Slee, 1993). These feelings stem, in part, from fears of retaliation (Musher-Eizenman et al., 2004), which often prevent bystanders from seeking help (Unnever and Cornell, 2003). Compared with their peers who have not observed bullying, individuals who have report more symptoms of interpersonal sensitivity, helplessness, and potential suicidal ideation (Rivers and Noret, 2013).

Limber reported that many have argued that prevalent bullying or bullying that is not adequately addressed within a school environment can contribute to a negative school climate (Espelage and Swearer, 2010; Olweus, 1993; Olweus et al., 2007), where *school climate* is defined as the quality and character of school life, including collective beliefs, values, and attitudes (Cohen, 2009; Cohen et al., 2009). Cohen et al. (2009) found that safety, including attitudes about bullying and violence, is one of four essential dimensions of school climate. Students who perceive staff members to be supportive are more likely to indicate they would seek help for bullying and threats of violence (Eliot et al., 2010). In addition, bullying prevention at schools has been associated not only with reductions in bullying but also with improvements in the social climate of the school (Olweus, 1991, 1997).

Finally, Limber said, bullying may result in substantial costs to society. Those who have been involved in bullying are "overconsumers" of society's health and social services (Olweus, 2012; Sourander et al., 2007), she said. For example, efforts to quantify the costs for troubled youth estimate that the cost of saving a single high-risk youth from a career in crime ranges from $2.6 million to $5.3 million (Cohen and Piquero, 2009; Cohen et al., 2010).

Future research will help to quantify the costs of bullying. But there is no doubt, Limber concluded, that "the individual human price tag is far too costly."

# 3

# Targets of Bullying and Bullying Behavior

---

**Key Points Made by Individual Speakers**

- Ethnic minority middle-school students generally feel safer and less bullied in more diverse contexts, perhaps because they perceive peer mistreatment as a sign of prejudice and do not blame themselves in the same way that majority students do. (Juvonen)
- Having one friend lowers the risk of being bullied, and even a neutral social interaction can help re-establish a sense of connection after being bullied. (Juvonen)
- Bullying has been associated with direct and indirect exposure to family violence and with sexual harassment and teen dating violence during adolescence. (Espelage)
- Many of the students who engage in bullying are found to be near the center of dense social networks, and aggression tends to stay within social categories. (Faris)
- Genetics research, neuroimaging, studies of the stress hormone cortisol, and investigations of chromosomal changes all have revealed harmful biological changes associated with bullying. (Vaillancourt)

Bullying can be analyzed at different levels, from the sociological to the genetic. In the initial panel of the workshop, four presenters summarized research on students who bully others and on the targets of bullying from four different perspectives and then, in the discussion period, explored possible ways in which these perspectives could be integrated.

## CONTEXTUAL EFFECTS ON THE TARGETS OF BULLYING

"Why are we concerned about bullying?" asked Jaana Juvonen, professor in the developmental psychology program at the University of California, Los Angeles. Is it because of its prevalence or because of the negative effects on the targets of bullying? The answer, in all likelihood, is both, she said. But when the effectiveness of interventions is examined, the focus is on prevalence and related factors, such as improvements in school climate. These outcomes are undoubtedly important, but Juvonen said that she was unable to find, in preparing for the workshop, even one study that examined whether anti-bullying efforts help alleviate the emotional pain and the health consequences for the most vulnerable—those who experience bullying repeatedly.

To create environments that protect the chronically bullied, it is necessary to understand how bullying-related distress varies across contexts and situations, Juvonen said. First, the emotional distress of the targeted varies across individuals. This variation is usually attributed to individual differences among the targets of bullying. For example, those who show more distress may be seen as lacking emotion-regulation abilities, being more sensitive to rejection, or not having good coping strategies, Juvonen said.

Much less is known, Juvonen said, about the role of social context. For example, how does group composition or the relationships in a particular context make the pain of bullying either greater or less? To address this void in the research, Juvonen and her colleague Sandra Graham have been investigating features of the social environments of school-based bullying to try to understand the links between bullying experiences and emotional distress. Specifically, they have compared the plight of targets of bullying across schools that vary in ethnic composition, with a focus on environments in which students feel safe as opposed to unsafe.

Comparing schools in California with varied ethnic compositions, they found that African-American and Latino middle-school students generally felt safer and less bullied in the more diverse contexts (Juvonen et al., 2006). However, Juvonen asked, although diversity may be protective for at least some groups or individuals, is there safety in numbers of similar others when bullied? Peer groups become increasingly ethnically segregated across grades, suggesting that same-ethnic peers are an important reference group. The question, then, she said, is whether the plight of a target may vary depending on the size of his or her ethnic group.

In this case, Juvonen and her colleagues examined social anxiety and found a stronger association between victimization and social anxiety when the victims of bullying had a greater number of same-ethnic peers (Bellmore et al., 2004). Similar findings were obtained for loneliness, she said. Thus, being bullied was more strongly associated with both social anxiety and loneliness when students were in settings with greater (as opposed to fewer) same-ethnic peers.

This finding raises the question of how targets construe their plight. When youth are bullied, Juvonen observed, they are likely to ask, "Why me?" Answers to this question—that is, the attributions they make—are likely to affect the level or type of distress they experience.

Using the construct of *characterological self-blame*—the idea that targets come to blame themselves and believe that there is nothing they can do about it—Juvonen and her colleagues looked at why students who belong to majority groups in their school would feel worse. They found a stronger association between getting bullied and self-blame when the students belonged to the numerical majority (Graham et al., 2009). In contrast, no association was found between bullying and self-blame when the students belonged to the numerical minority in their schools. Recent evidence suggests that those who are in the numerical minority perceive this kind of peer mistreatment as reflecting prejudice on the part of their peers and do not blame themselves in the same way that those who belong to the numerical majority, Juvonen said.

To further understand the role of characterological self-blame, Juvonen and her colleagues have more recently examined its potential role in prolonging bullying. Focusing on the first year in middle school, they looked at which youths bullied in the fall continued to be targeted by the spring of sixth grade. The question was whether self-blame functions similarly to depression—as both a consequence and a risk factor of victimization. They found support for indirect associations, in that children who had been targeted in the beginning of sixth grade were more likely to continue to be bullied throughout the school year if they self-blamed and become depressed (Schacter et al., 2014).

These analyses suggest that contextual factors affect how children interpret their mistreatment and that self-blame is especially detrimental, Juvonen said. They also suggest that to alleviate distress and reduce the duration of bullying, interventions may need to change targets' attributions of their plight.

### The Power of Friends

Juvonen concluded her presentation with "something a little more positive." A particularly potent protective factor against bullying, she said, is having friends. Although the type of friend matters, good evidence suggests that having even one friend lowers the risk of being bullied. Moreover, when a student is bullied, his or her distress can be alleviated by having that one friend, Juvonen said.

Two recent dissertation studies from her laboratory provide further insights about these findings, suggesting that the effect may result not from individual differences in whether children have friends but from social replenishment after peer mistreatment. In the first study, Guadalupe Espinoza showed that when an individual experienced cyberbullying, time spent with friends—not the quality of the friendship—alleviated the intensity of distress reported by high school students (Espinoza, under review). If, on the day a student was cyberbullied, that student spent some time with a friend, stress was significantly and substantially alleviated, Juvonen said.

In the second study, Elisheva Gross varied the activities of youth who were excluded in an online experiment: They were randomly assigned either to instant message with an unknown peer or to play a solitary computer game. The goal was to document recovery from self-esteem loss related to the exclusion experience. What she found was that recovery was much quicker for those who had a chance to interact with an unknown peer as opposed to playing a solitary computer game (Gross, 2009). These findings suggest that recovery does not even "require" having a friend but just connecting with a peer, Juvonen observed.

This research has helped identify two possible antidotes to bullying that can vary across situations and contexts, Juvonen said. The first is to realize "It's not just me" in thinking about bullying. The second is to recognize that even a neutral social interaction can help reestablish a sense of connection after being bullied. It is important to realize that environments make youth socially isolated, Juvonen said. Youth are not socially isolated unless other people ignore or exclude them, she said, which is why a school environment that fosters connectedness is critically important.

## ASSOCIATIONS AMONG BULLYING, SEXUAL HARASSMENT, AND DATING VIOLENCE

Bullying is not an isolated behavior, observed Dorothy Espelage, Edward William Gutgsell and Jane Marr Gutgsell Endowed Professor in the Department of Educational Psychology at the University of Illinois, Urbana-Champaign. For example, several cross-sectional and a handful of longitudinal studies link direct and indirect exposure to family violence with bullying behavior (Espelage et al., 2000, 2013; Voisin and Hong, 2012). Bullying is also predictive of sexual violence during adolescence, and the two share similar risk factors (Basile et al., 2009; Espelage et al., 2012). In addition, Miller et al. (2013) demonstrate how dating violence and bullying often co-occur, highlighting the need to recognize the interrelatedness of these behaviors.

However, few longitudinal studies have unpacked the mechanisms from the contextual variables of bully perpetration, Espelage said. Even fewer longitudinal studies have considered how bully perpetration is associated with the emergence of gender-based bullying, sexual harassment, or teen dating violence during early adolescence.

Espelage and her colleagues (2014) have proposed a developmental model of bullying, sexual harassment, and dating violence. To test this model, they tracked 1,162 racially and economically diverse students from 2008 to 2013. The students were in three cohorts—fifth, sixth, and seventh graders in 2008—with seven waves of data collection occurring during the years of the study.

One takeaway message from this research, Espelage said, is that homophobic name-calling and unwanted sexual commentary are prevalent in middle school. "It takes about 3 minutes when you go into a middle school to hear this kind of language," she said. Youth who engage in bullying behavior resort to homophobic name-calling over the middle-school years (Espelage et al., 2012, in press). Boys and girls may try to demonstrate their heterosexuality by sexually harassing others. Bullying and homophobic name-calling may also promote unhealthy dating relationships, she said.

This has been a powerful finding for teachers and administrators, who say that they often hear this language. Bullying prevention programs need to include a discussion of language that marginalizes gender non-conforming and lesbian, gay, bisexual, and transgender youth, Espelage said, despite the potential backlash from those who see such discussions as promoting an alternative sexual orientation.

Espelage's research also has demonstrated that bullying and homophobic name-calling is associated with later sexual harassment (Espelage et al., in press). As students transition to high school, a strong connection emerges between bullying and sexual harassment, she said. In addition, sexual harassment, unwanted sexual commentary, and unwanted touching predicted teen dating violence, including verbal, physical, and sexual coercion.

This research is predicated on a social–ecological model and a social–interactional learning model in which family violence serves as an important context for understanding the relations among bullying perpetration, sexual harassment perpetration, and teen dating violence, Espelage explained. The researchers have tested this model by evaluating the changing influence of key social agents across early to late adolescence. For example, in the dataset discussed by Espelage at the workshop, 32 risk and protective factors were considered. Girls were separated out because of the tremendous variability in the ways in which they report bullying perpetration and exposure to family conflict and sibling aggression. On this last point, Espelage noted that sibling aggression is emerging as a potent predictor of bullying involvement for both perpetration and victimization. For boys, family conflict did not predict bullying perpetration, just sibling aggression. "Sibling aggression, which many of us feel is a proxy in some ways for violence in the home, was an important predictor here as well," Espelage said.

### Possible Next Steps

From this research, Espelage offered several suggestions. Future research will need to consider multiple contexts to identify longitudinal predictors, mediators, and moderators associated with outcomes for youth who engage in bullying behavior, she said. "We must begin to think much more creatively about incorporating discussions of gender-based name-calling, sexual violence, and gender expression."

In addition, Espelage said there is a need to examine and respond to various forms of interpersonal violence as a part of prevention of bullying and youth violence. In particular, Espelage pointed to exposure to family violence and teen-dating violence victimization and perpetration. Such research could evaluate the changing influence of key socializing agents across early to late adolescence and examine the antecedents, correlates, and sequelae of bullying, sexual harassment, and teen dating violence, she said.

Finally, Espelage said that there is a need for comprehensive, social–ecological longitudinal studies to understand the complex developmental unfolding of different types of youth violence. The effect sizes for many bullying prevention programs have been low and have even been negative for some programs in high schools, partly because programs designed for elementary school children are being used inappropriately for older students (Yeager et al., in press). "We need to be developmentally sensitive to the types of experiences kids are reporting," Espelage said.

## INSTRUMENTAL AGGRESSION

The research literature on bullying suggests that individuals who engage in bullying behavior have two contradictory attributes, said Robert Faris, associate professor of sociology at the University of California, Davis. On the one hand, bully perpetrators would seem to have substantial forms of maladjustment, such as troubled home lives or challenging psychological dispositions, which would imply that they are on the fringes of social networks and do not have high status. On the other hand, he said, bullying would seem to be a way of building status by establishing one's place in a social hierarchy.

Faris's own research suggests that both of these observations are accurate. "I find a lot of evidence to suggest a very traditional perspective of maladjusted kids who are picking on those who are weaker than them," he said. "I also found a second pattern, . . . which is instrumental aggression."[1] When the social connections among students in a high school are diagrammed, many of the students who engage in bullying are found to be near the center of dense social networks, Faris said. Connections between individuals who engage in bullying behavior and their targets tend not to occur around the perimeter of social networks, as the early work on bullying would suggest (Faris, 2012). "What we see is a preponderance of ties originating within the core of these networks among the more popular kids," he said. "I think this is evidence of an instrumental pattern of aggression."

Working with Susan Ennett, Faris has also done research on the role of status motivation. They found that students who want to be more popular are more aggressive (Faris and Ennett, 2012). They also found that students, regardless of how much they care about popularity themselves, are more likely to be aggressive if they have friends who care about popularity. In addition, they found that the highest rates of aggression occur between pairs of students who are both high status, not between high-status and low-status students. "To me that is consistent with the idea of competition for status and the use of aggression to those ends," Faris said.

## Social Distance

Instrumental aggression also depends in part on social distance.[2] Aggression tends to stay within social categories, Faris said. For example, the highest rates of aggression tend to be within race and not across race. His data indicate that bullying has a very low likelihood of crossing racial lines.

The situation with gender is similar: The highest rates of aggression are between girls and between boys rather than across gender lines. Although boys and girls have roughly equal rates of aggression, both boys and girls target girls more often than they target boys, which results in girls being disproportionately targeted, Faris said.

---

[1] Instrumental aggression refers to purposive aggression intended to achieve some goal, particularly higher social status.

[2] Social distance can refer to fundamental demographic barriers (e.g., racial divides) and, in social network terms, to the number of friendship links separating two people in a social network (e.g., a friend of a friend is distance 2).

Working with a different dataset, Faris and his colleagues found very high rates of aggression among adolescents who identify as lesbian, gay, bisexual, transgender, or questioning (LGBTQ) as well as the more traditional pattern of heterosexual students bullying LGBTQ youth at a relatively high rate (see Figure 3-1). Again, he said, bullying often occurs within social demographics.

Faris said that a similar conclusion also emerges from analyses of friendship networks. Rates of bullying drop dramatically as young people become farther apart socially. A lot of aggression occurs within friendship groups and even between friends, Faris said. This can lead to some complicated dynamics. For example, preliminary evidence suggests that when friends have an aggressive event, they cease to become friends. But when two students who are not friends are aggressive toward each other, they have a greater likelihood of becoming friends at some point in the future. "There is a cycle of conflict that is going on," Faris said "Allegiances are being formed and broken up."

Cyberbullying appears to exhibit the same patterns, Faris said. Relatively high-status students are more likely to target each other.

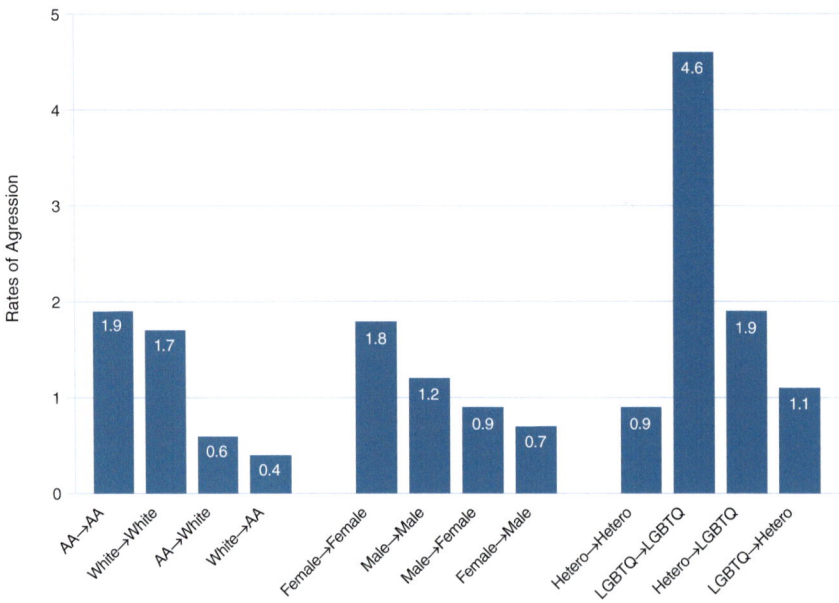

**FIGURE 3-1** Aggression rates are higher within race, gender, and sexual orientation categories than across categories.
NOTE: AA = African American; LGBTQ = lesbian, gay, bisexual, transgender, or questioning.
SOURCE: Faris presentation, 2014.

In a recent paper, Faris and his colleagues looked at five different outcomes of victimization: anger, anxiety, depression, attachment to school, and centrality in social networks, which they referred to as status (Faris and Felmlee, 2014). They found that the victims who were high status had a more adverse reaction to aggression. When high-status students are victimized, their anger, anxiety, and depression increase much more dramatically than is the case with lower-status students, and they drop in status much more than do low-status students—an effect that is also seen with students who are in the middle of social hierarchies. By the time students reach high school, a given act of bullying is not necessarily going to transform the sense of self of a low-status student, Faris said, but "a kid who may have struggled mightily to reach a lofty social position might experience a little more distress. They may feel that they have more to lose."

### Is Bullying Instrumental?

The final issue Faris discussed was whether bullying is effective if it is considered as instrumental. The data suggest that victims of bullying do lose status. In addition, using yearbook data to provide additional measures of social status, Faris and his colleagues found that aggressive behavior predicted a significant increase in social status by the end of high school, but it depended partly on whom was targeted (Faris, 2012). "They had to go after kids who were socially close, kids who were themselves aggressive, or kids who were high status themselves," he said. "They had to pick the right targets to receive a social boost. Again, I think this all fits a picture of aggression as at least potentially useful for climbing social ladders."

In general, these data point to a relatively poor quality of friendships among high school students and adolescents, Faris said. As an example of these poor-quality friendships, he noted that if students are asked to name their eight best friends, only 37 percent of those ties are reciprocated. Furthermore, when Faris and his colleagues asked students to name their five closest friends every 2 weeks, they found high rates of turnover in those lists.

"This is a symptom of a problem," he said. "It is related to this process of competing for status. If we thought about ways of helping kids develop stronger, more robust friendships and perhaps fewer of them, I think that might help build resilience."

Many young people do not recognize what a good friend is and do not know how to be a good friend, Faris said. Parents and other adults can help teach these lessons, he said, and schools could be reorganized to offer activities that can foster interest-based friendships, as opposed to their traditional organization of offering just a few prestigious activities, he suggested.

## THE BIOLOGICAL MECHANISMS ASSOCIATED WITH BULLYING

Some youth fare poorly when they are bullied, and some do better. It is important to understand the moderators and mediators behind this variability, said Tracy Vaillancourt, a professor and the Canada Research Chair in Children's Mental Health and Violence Prevention at the University of Ottawa. For example, she said, some evidence suggests that girls are profoundly affected by being socially excluded, while boys are more affected by being physically abused by their peers. Social support also matters. For example, children who are targets of bullying at school and also experience bullying at home tend to have poorer outcomes. In addition, temperament is associated with how people cope with stress, in that some people are more agitated over time, Vaillancourt said.

Less attention has been paid to the biological moderators and mediators that are associated with bullying at a physiological level, Vaillancourt said. She summarized research in four areas of "how bullying gets under the skin to confer risk."

### Genetic Evidence

Genetic evidence suggests that biology may confer a risk for poorer outcomes. Caspi et al. (2003) found that a polymorphism of a serotonin transporter gene influenced the likelihood of a person being depressed at age 26 after having been severely maltreated, probably maltreated, or not maltreated in childhood. Those who had been severely maltreated and who had two short alleles for the gene had a depression rate of about 70 percent at age 26, while those who had been severely maltreated and who had two long alleles had no greater odds of being depressed at age 26 than children who had been treated well by their caregivers, Vaillancourt said.

This study has been replicated within the context of peer abuse, Vaillancourt said. Looking at girls who have been relationally victimized by their peers, Benjet et al. (2010) found that having the short allele of the gene conferred a risk of depression that was three times greater than having the long allele. "I can't think of something that confers such a strong risk," Vaillancourt said. This "is a really powerful finding."

### Neurophysiological Evidence

People who have experienced bullying often use physical pain metaphors to describe the social pain they feel. Such comments as, "It felt like somebody punched me in the stomach," or "It broke my heart when they said that to me," are common, Vaillancourt said.

Neuroscience points to an overlap between social and physical pain,

Vaillancourt said. For example, Chen et al. (2008) found that people can relive and re-experience social pain more easily than physical pain and that the emotions they feel are more intense and painful than the experience of physical pain. "Physical pain is short-lived, whereas social pain can last a lifetime," Vaillancourt said. "Think about when you were in grade six and you were excluded or ostracized. Then think about the time when maybe you broke your ankle. When you think about breaking your ankle, you don't get a visceral reaction to recalling the event. When you recall the event of being excluded by the peer group, it is as if you are living it today."

Neuroimaging studies show that parts of the cortical physical pain network are activated when a person is socially excluded (Masten et al., 2009). The same areas of the brain that are activated when a person stubs a toe are activated when that person is called stupid or is not invited to a party, Vaillancourt said.

Similarly, children may be hypersensitive to rejection, Vaillancourt said. Crowley et al. (2009) found that 12-year-olds could recognize being rejected in less than 500 milliseconds. "We have this radar . . . to not being included," she said, which might have its roots in some evolutionary advantages in mammalian species.

### Neuroendocrine Evidence

A large amount of research has examined the hypothalamic/pituitary/adrenal (HPA) axis, or the human body's stress system, Vaillancourt said. One product of that stress system is cortisol, which has been used as a biomarker of dysregulation of the HPA axis—that is, of impairments in the normal functioning of the HPA system.

When people are stressed, they produce more cortisol, which has been shown to have detrimental effects on the brain, Vaillancourt explained. However, she added, when people face extreme and prolonged stress, cortisol levels tend to be lower than normal, perhaps because receptor sites are damaged from cortisol overproduction.

A variety of studies have demonstrated a link between peer victimization and dysregulation of the HPA axis, Vaillancourt said. Dysregulation of the HPA axis has also been shown to be related to disruptions in neurogenesis, or the growth of new brain cells, resulting in poorer memory. For example, Vaillancourt et al. (2011) found that children who were victimized by their peers became depressed, and this depression led to changes in the HPA axis. The dysregulation of the HPA axis led in turn to memory deficits, particularly in areas that are sensitive to the effects of cortisol. "One of the things that we know about kids who are bullied is that they don't do as well in school," Vaillancourt said. "A lot of times we think that perhaps it has to do with the fact that they are distracted by being bullied, [but] perhaps the effects of being bullied are affecting their memory, which then changes their academic profile and outcomes."

In a study of whether changes in the HPA axis are actually caused by having been bullied, Ouellet-Morin et al. (2011) looked at pairs of identical twins, one of whom experienced bullying and the other of whom did not. The researchers showed that these childhood experiences had a causal effect on the neuroendocrine response to stress. "It is not the case that kids get bullied because for some reason the peer group picks up on the fact that their HPA axis is different and that they are dysregulated. They become dysregulated as a function of being bullied," Vaillancourt said.

### Telomere Erosion

Finally, Vaillancourt described the erosion of telomeres, which are repetitive DNA sections at the ends of chromosomes that promote chromosomal stability and help regulate the replicative lifespan of cells. The length of telomeres is linked to normal processes such as aging and is associated with such health behaviors as smoking and obesity. "Your telomere gets shorter and shorter the longer you live and the more bad things you do," Vaillancourt explained.

Shalev et al. (2013) recently found that exposure to violence during childhood, including bullying, was associated with telomere erosion from 5 to 10 years of age. These changes could alter a person's developmental or health trajectory through epigenetic mechanisms and explain, for example, why one sister develops breast cancer while her twin sister does not, Vaillancourt said.

### Changing Health Trajectories

Understanding the biological underpinnings of how peer relations affect emotional and physical health can help legitimize the plight of peer-abused children and youth, Vaillancourt concluded. It can also cause policy makers and practitioners to prioritize the reduction of school bullying. These kinds of findings "urge us to really get going," she said, because bullying and bullying prevention can change children's health trajectories.

### INTEGRATING PERSPECTIVES

During the discussion period, several questions centered on the issue of integrating the different perspectives offered by the four presenters in this session. In response to a question on this subject, Vaillancourt said that one of her motivations in studying bullying is to prevent the targets of bullying from being re-victimized by educators who think that they are at fault and just need to be tougher. If some students are shown to be biologically more susceptible to the negative effects of bullying, then principals, parents, and other adults may be less likely to blame the targets of bullying and more likely to protest strongly when students are bullied.

Vaillancourt also described recent epigenetics research that points to changes in the expression of genes as a consequence of environmental influences, including early adversity. "We have failed to recognize that the stress of being bullied by our peers, which interferes with our fundamental need to belong, would be equivalent to living in a house where you are abused by your caregiver," she said. "It would be equivalent to living in extreme poverty." The study of epigenetic effects caused by such experiences may be a way to understand mental and physical health trajectories. "We all need to come together and intersect our knowledge bases so that we can be better informed in preventing this," she said.

Espelage said that her longitudinal study found that not only was bullying perpetration predicted by family violence but also bully perpetration and victimization were associated with the later onset of alcohol and drug use in the victims (Espelage et al., 2013; Rao et al., in press). Faris observed that the victims of bullying are more likely to turn to substance use as a way of coping.

The moderator of the panel, Catherine Bradshaw of the University of Virginia, speculated that aggressors may be picking up on the emotional vulnerability of some individuals and targeting them and that students who are less affected by bullying may be less attractive targets. Perhaps individuals engaging in bullying behavior use social cues and the reactivity of other students to choose targets, Bradshaw suggested.

Vaillancourt pointed to recent research on how the presence or absence of power affects the brain (Hogeveen et al., 2014). When a subject is afforded power, he or she pays less attention to and is less aroused by others. At the neurological level, those who hold power are less sensitive to the plight of others. Those who do not hold power are much more aware of the environment and the distress signals of others, Vaillancourt said.

One of the youth panelists, Glenn Cantave, a junior at Wesley University, noted that when he was younger he was more sensitive to the attacks of bullies, but he has since developed a "thicker skin." Does that, he asked, imply some sort of tolerance to stress that perhaps would be related to cortisol levels?

Vaillancourt responded that the offspring of Holocaust survivors have lower cortisol levels, even though they did not experience the trauma of the Holocaust themselves. Perhaps such lower cortisol levels are a protective adaptation that acts to reduce the risks associated with chronically high cortisol levels, but the actual mechanisms behind the lowered cortisol levels are still not well understood. For example, Vaillancourt said, almost every study of children who have been bullied finds that they have low cortisol, whereas their longitudinal studies showed first high levels and then low levels, suggesting that the dysregulation of cortisol is a more important factor to look for than absolute levels. Longitudinal studies of the HPA axis over time across different stressors could reveal some of the mechanisms behind these complex patterns, she suggested.

Vaillancourt also referred back to the relationship between depression and being bullied. The depression often comes first, suggesting that the lack of engagement among depressed young people may make them more vulnerable to victimization. Again, she said, longitudinal studies would help explain the observed heterogeneity in trajectories and outcomes.

Basing interventions on the social organization of schools may be a way to integrate knowledge in practice. For example, Espelage pointed out that a better approach than universal programs for sexual violence and rape prevention might be to identify students who have the greatest social capital and train them to be attitude changers, drawing on what is known from industrial and organizational psychology. Bystander intervention programs have been shown to produce large effect sizes in promoting positive bystander behaviors (Polanin et al., 2012), she said. Another promising approach is to work with teachers to understand the networks and hierarchies in their classrooms.

Juvonen agreed that focusing on bystanders is an especially promising way of changing the high status of individuals who engage in bullying behavior. "Bullies love the audience," she said. "They want not only a reaction from their victim, but they also live for the fact that everybody else is in awe and joins the bully rather than the victim. It is those dynamics that need to be changed." One way to turn this around, Juvonen suggested, may be to emphasize to students the rights that they have, one of which is the right to come to school and not be afraid.

Juvonen also pointed out that teachers and administrators know who the lowest-ranking individuals are—and thus have a good idea of those who are at highest risk for victimization—yet not many schools offer proactive remedies for these students. Instead, a wise librarian or well-liked teacher might keep a door open after lunch. A better option, Juvonen said, would be a lunchroom that brings people together with specific interests. "We have a lot of smart teachers and educators out there who are doing little things that can make a huge difference."

# Part II

# Contexts for Prevention and Intervention

# 4

# School-Based Interventions

> **Key Points Made by Individual Speakers**
> - Research has identified some effective elements of anti-bullying initiatives, including high levels of playground supervision, rules related to bullying, the training of teachers, and the involvement of parents. (Bradshaw)
> - Research has also identified approaches that are not recommended, including zero-tolerance policies, grouping aggressive youth together, and brief awareness campaigns. (Bradshaw)
> - School climate factors that can affect problem behaviors among students include student-to-teacher ratios and the number of different students taught by the typical teacher, a sense of community or belonging in a school, and consistent discipline management that supports positive school norms. (Gottfredson)
> - Recent school violence has led to a spate of new school safety measures, but these steps can cost millions of dollars and can deprive schools of resources that could be allocated to anti-bullying programs and counseling services. (Cornell)

Schools are one important setting in which bullying among youth occurs. They are also where many of the interventions designed to prevent or ameliorate the effects of bullying are implemented. In the first of six panels on anti-bullying initiatives in specific contexts, three presenters examined the aspects of schools that can facilitate or prevent bullying and the key elements of effective school-based programs.

## SCHOOL-BASED PREVENTIVE INTERVENTIONS

As indicated in the previous chapter, bullying is a particular form of aggressive behavior, but it also is part of a broader set of problem behaviors seen within schools. Programs designed to prevent both bullying and these other problem behaviors have been studied, and the results can be applied either narrowly to bullying or else more broadly, observed Catherine Bradshaw, a professor and the associate dean for research and faculty development at the University of Virginia Curry School of Education.

Ttofi and Farrington (2011) carried out a meta-analysis of 53 rigorous evaluations and randomized trials of programs aimed at preventing bullying, two-thirds of which were conducted outside of the United States and Canada. They found overall a 23 percent decrease in the perpetration of bullying and a 20 percent decrease in victimization. The most effective elements of programs that they identified were:

- use of parent training activities, meetings, and information
- high levels of playground supervision
- use of consistent disciplinary methods
- classroom management strategies
- classroom and school-wide rules related to bullying
- training of teachers (including aspects of that training and the amount of time and intensity of training)
- multicomponent prevention approaches

Some caveats should be noted concerning this meta-analysis, Bradshaw said. First, the effects generally were stronger in the nonrandomized controlled trial designs. Impacts were also larger among older children, and the programs generally were more effective in European than in North American sites.

Some observers, such as Merrell et al. (2008), have argued that there are relatively few effective universal bullying prevention programs. To examine this issue, Bradshaw and her colleagues have been looking more broadly at violence prevention efforts. School-wide efforts that involve all school staff and are implemented across all school settings show the most promise in reducing bullying and rejection, she said. For example, a model called KiVa developed in Finland shares some elements of school-wide approaches (Salmivalli et al., 2011). It uses a videogame that students can use to practice different strategies in resolving bullying situations. That model is now being studied to determine whether cultural and contextual changes need to be made to it in order for it to be imported successfully into the United States, Bradshaw said.

Universal school-wide prevention models that are broadly focused on violence and disruptive behaviors may also affect bullying, she said. For example, frameworks based on social–emotional learning have demonstrated effectiveness in some cases, although not in others. One example of a successful program is Second Step, which was originally developed for elementary school but more recently has been extended to middle school; it has had some promising effects on precursors to bullying behavior. Similarly, the PATHS (Promoting Alternative Thinking Strategies) program has been shown to affect a wide range of behavioral and mental health outcomes, Bradshaw said.

Programs that focus on classroom management may also be effective in reducing problem behaviors, including bullying, Bradshaw said. For example, studies in Baltimore by Sheppard Kellam and Nick Ialongo have shown that just 1 year of implementation of a classroom management strategy called the Good Behavior Game can produce long-term effects across a range of outcomes, including substance use, violent and aggressive behaviors, and bullying (Kellam et al., 2011). This research has also found effects on academic performance, high school completion, and the number of students who need special education services. "That is one model of classroom management that we could think about more broadly as it relates to impacting bullying and other outcomes," Bradshaw said.

A public health approach to prevention is one way to build a multi-tiered system of support, Bradshaw said. This approach combines universal prevention for all students with indicated or intensive intervention for a few students and selective or targeted interventions for some additional students. Research has demonstrated that these approaches can have significant impacts on the school environment, Bradshaw said, including significant improvements in school climate and systems changes that are sustainable over multiple years. For example, data from randomized, controlled trials of a model known as the Positive Behavior Support Framework found significant reductions of suspensions as well as bullying behavior, she said.

Bradshaw concluded by recommending that bullying prevention programs contain the following core elements:

- Teacher training
- Activities for students
- Parent activities
- Multi-component programs

- School-wide scope
- Continuum of positive supports
- Data-driven process

Bradshaw also touched on several approaches that are not recommended. One example is a zero-tolerance policy in which students are automatically suspended for bullying. Another is to group students who bully together, because that can make their aggression worse rather than better, she said. Brief assemblies or 1-day awareness campaigns have little effect in terms of sustained outcomes for youth. Conflict resolution and peer mediation can be effective for other forms of aggressive behavior but raise concerns in the context of bullying. Finally, focusing excessively on issues of mental health and suicide can contribute to contagion processes rather than addressing the problem directly, Bradshaw said.

In multi-component programs, it is important to provide training to classroom teachers concerning classroom management and what to do in bullying situations. "It sounds like a no-brainer," she said, "but there are programs that don't actually provide any training to teachers." Similarly, while parent engagement is a clear challenge for nearly all schools, school–home communication about bullying is particularly important in order to let parents and caregivers know about the strategies and lessons being taught in school, she said. Multi-component programs are characterized by a continuum of responses, so that suspending a student is not the only option, but rather an array of positively oriented activities exists from which to choose, Bradshaw said.

In response to a question about the use of conflict-resolution centers to provide free confidential mediations to people in the community who need it, including students and teachers, Bradshaw responded that schools need to have many tools in their toolkits. The same tools used to deal with conflicts or fights may not be useful in a bullying situation. Many youths who are victimized by their peers do not want to sit across the table and talk with their aggressors, even in a well-structured environment. But many other strategies exist, such as restorative practices where youth can make up for past transgressions. Systematic research is needed to determine which of these interventions work best in different circumstances, she said.

In response to a later question about playground supervision and whether the lack of unstructured play may be inhibiting the development of conflict-resolution skills, Bradshaw pointed to the importance of youths learning how to resolve small day-to-day conflicts as practice for larger conflicts. "That way when it does get big, you have some kind of skill set to draw upon." Similarly, social–emotional curricula seek to give students strategies and skills for learning how to label and regulate their own emotions, she said.

## SCHOOL CLIMATE AND BULLYING

Schools are more than the sum of the individuals inhabiting those schools, said Denise Gottfredson, professor in the Department of Criminal Justice and Criminology at the University of Maryland. Each school has its own personality, and that personality influences student outcomes, including the amount and nature of bullying in a school.

Gottfredson pointed to research dating back to the 1970s that demonstrated the importance of three aspects of the school climate in predicting a variety of problem behaviors among students:

- Student-to-teacher ratio
- School norms
- Consistent discipline (Cook et al., 2010b)

Regarding student-to-teacher ratios, in the 1970s the Safe School Study, which looked at a national sample of 642 secondary schools, identified several school climate predictors of victimization, one of which was large schools (Gottfredson and Gottfredson, 1985). More recently, Gottfredson and DiPietro (2011) used data from the National Study of Delinquency Prevention in Schools to try to replicate that finding and also to explore other measures related to school size. They found that higher student-to-teacher ratios and a higher number of different students taught by typical teachers increased student victimization, replicating the findings from the Safe School Study. However, they found that higher overall student enrollment was related to lower victimization rates, Gottfredson said, suggesting that it is not the total number of students in a school that matters but the ratio of students to teachers and the ways that students are organized for instruction. Similarly, a recent study of 95 elementary schools found that students in schools with higher student-to-teacher ratios reported greater frequencies of bully victimization and reduced perceptions of safety (Bradshaw et al., 2009).

The second factor involves a sense of community or of belonging in a school, part of which involves a shared belief about acceptable behaviors. In their study of schools, Gottfredson and DiPietro (2011) found that one reason why students in schools with higher ratios of students to teachers experience more victimization is that these schools have less consensus regarding norms for behavior. Gottfredson's colleague Allison Payne, using the National Study Data, further demonstrated the importance of a communal social organization, in which students and adults know, care about, and support one another, have common goals and a sense of shared purpose, and actively contribute and feel personally committed to the school. Payne found that a communal social organization reduces student delinquency and that the effects of this factor on delinquency are mediated by student bonding (Payne et al., 2003). Students in schools with communal social organizations are more attached to school, and that attachment serves to inhibit their offending behavior. Similarly, a recent study of nearly 300 schools found that students in schools with high levels of perceived teacher and school staff support are more willing to seek help for bullying and aggressive behavior (Eliot et al., 2010).

The third factor Gottfredson highlighted is consistent discipline management that supports school norms. A study done in the 1990s by the U.S. Department of Education and the National Institute of Justice found that consistent discipline management was related to lower levels of student victimization and delinquency (Gottfredson et al., 2005). That study also found that a more positive social climate—as measured by organizational focus, teacher morale, and strong administrator leadership—was related to lower levels of teacher victimization. A more recent analysis similarly demonstrated that teacher support and firm and consistent discipline management are related to lower levels of both bullying and other forms of victimization (Gregory et al., 2010).

To her discussion of these three factors, Gottfredson added a brief description of a study undertaken to understand what factors might have led to the spate of school shootings experienced in the 1990s. This study sent teams of ethnographers into six different communities that had experienced lethal school shootings to interview people and to collect records relevant to the incidents. The study is relevant to bullying because many of the shooters reported feeling bullied at school, Gottfredson said. The most relevant finding from this study for purposes of understanding bullying was that there was a large gulf between youth and adults in these communities (IOM and NRC, 2003). The study found that the adults had a very poor understanding of the children's experiences. The study also found that shooters reported that they felt they had nowhere to turn, that they were intensely concerned about their status and protecting themselves, and that specific warnings had been given and missed. All of this research demonstrates the importance of meaningful relationships between students and the adults in a school, Gottfredson said.

Gottfredson summarized the research on the several interventions to improve the aspects of school climate that she had discussed earlier. Although the quality of the research on these interventions is generally low by current standards (e.g., most of the studies were not randomized controlled trials [ERCTs]), these trials nevertheless provide promising results for reasonable interventions that could be tested more rigorously today, she said.

## Changing School Climates

In the 1980s the Office of Juvenile Justice and Delinquency Prevention funded tests of 16 different ideas on how to intervene in schools to prevent delinquency, with two of these programs focusing on changing aspects of a school's climate related to bullying, Gottfredson said. Although the studies do not meet the standards of rigor used today, they provide promising ideas that could be revisited and tested more rigorously, she said.

The first program, Project STATUS, reorganized schools using a school within a school approach (Gottfredson, 1990). The schools used block scheduling to create a 2-hour block of time that was team-taught by program teachers who were especially trained to use more engaging teaching methods. For at least this portion of the day, students stayed with the same teachers and with the same group of students in a small environment that was designed to promote a sense of belonging and cooperation. An evaluation of the program indicated that it was successful in reducing various forms of problem behavior, including crime, antisocial behavior, and substance use, Gottfredson said.

The second program, Project PATHE, focused on reorganizing schools to improve students' attitudes about school. Schools were reorganized into teams of staff, students, and community members who worked together to revise school policies and practices in five different areas (Gottfredson, 1986, 1990). Two of these areas were the discipline policy and school climate. A discipline policy team focused on developing a referral system for discipline; developing handbooks that were distributed to students, parents, and staff; and focusing on consistent enforcement of that discipline policy, Gottfredson said. The school climate team worked on developing and implementing a variety of different activities throughout the school year that engaged students in fun and constructive activities, such as school pride campaigns and a variety of extracurricular activities. The program placed a great deal of emphasis on discipline management and a sense of belonging in the school. In a study involving nine schools over 2 years, evaluations showed that the program was successful at reducing a number of problem behaviors, she reported.

In addition to these older programs, several recent efforts, while not focused exclusively on bullying, have focused on aspects of school climate that are related to bullying, Gottfredson said. The first is Safe Dates, which is a dating violence prevention program for middle- and high-school students. It includes a 10-session curriculum as well as a theater production that is put on by the students about how an adolescent victim of dating violence can seek help, she explained. The program also includes a school-wide poster contest in which students develop posters about dating violence. The posters are displayed throughout the school, students vote on the best poster, and the three best posters win a cash prize. An RCT of the program in 14 schools found that it was effective for reducing psychological perpetration, sexual violence, and violence perpetrated against a current dating partner (Foshee et al., 2005).

Finally, Gottfredson said, the Positive Behavior Interventions and Supports (PBIS) program focuses on improving the school discipline system by creating a team of school community members who work together to improve the school over time. The team establishes expectations for positive behaviors, sets up positive reinforcement systems, and improves the clarity and consistency of discipline in the school. An RCT studying the school-wide components of PBIS in 37 schools found improved organizational health, reduced aggressive behavior, and reduced peer rejection (Bradshaw et al., 2008).

## Research Gaps

Taking into account the research that has been done to date, Gottfredson pointed to three areas of research that should be considered in the future. The first, she said, is to combine ideas from earlier and more recent school climate research in order to design more effective programs. The second is to rigorously test those programs. And the third is to examine how school climate influences the effectiveness of individually targeted interventions.

## BULLYING AND SCHOOL SAFETY

School policies on bullying are not carried out in a vacuum, observed Dewey Cornell, a forensic clinical psychologist and the Linda Bunker Professor of Education at the University of Virginia Curry School of Education. The policies are implemented in the context of broader school safety concerns that can be quite pressing and that can impede efforts to implement bullying prevention programs.

Since the 1990s broad school safety policies have been shaped extensively by fears of school violence, Cornell said. Today, school administrators have to consider building security, school shooting drills, zero-tolerance practices, and the pressure for high-stakes testing, all of which they see as competing priorities.

Recent school shootings have brought bullying to national attention because of a perceived link between bullying and these shootings, which has provided an important context for bullying prevention programs, Cornell said. A study of school shootings by the U.S. Secret Service and the U.S. Department of Education (2002) found that the majority of attackers felt bullied or persecuted. School shootings have seemingly transformed school safety and discipline, primarily through the expansion of zero-tolerance policies to not only firearms but also all sorts of toys and otherwise innocuous behaviors (Cornell, 2006). Today, schools are suspending students for much less serious behaviors than in the past, raising concerns about possible discriminatory practices, Cornell said. In general, events such as the Sandy Hook shootings have exposed people throughout society to terrible images, thoughts, and fears, which have strongly influenced school practices, he said. Since those shootings, some schools have rushed to institute security measures such as bulletproof building entrances, metal detectors, x-ray screening, cameras, and increased school security personnel, Cornell said. Other responses that have been discussed include giving teachers firearms training or putting additional locks on doors to keep out intruders with a gun, Cornell said.

These steps can cost millions of dollars, which can deprive schools of resources that could be allocated to anti-bullying programs and counseling services (DeAngelis et al., 2011). "It is a terrible dilemma to have to choose between security and anti-bullying," Cornell said. These security measures also have an impact on school climate, he said. It is unclear how these drills affect children's sense of security and their impact on school climate.

## Increases in School Safety

The new concern with school safety may be an overreaction, Cornell said. Homicides in which school-age youths are the victims rarely occur at school (see Figure 4-1). Instead, he said, most homicides occur in residences and at other locations, and school violence has actually declined over time. According to data from the Centers for Disease Control and Prevention, 98 to 99 percent of homicides of school-age children occur outside of school (CDC, 2014a,b; Modzeleski et al., 2008). But school shootings are so traumatic that they skew perceptions of school safety and convince the public and policy makers that there are urgent needs for security measures, Cornell said.

Overall, school-associated violent deaths—not only among students, but also staff members and adults as well—have been declining, Cornell said. One recent study estimated that the average school in the United States can expect a student homicide about once every 6,000 years (Borum et al., 2010). School violence has also declined, with aggravated assault, robbery, and forcible rape dropping substantially since the 1990s, Cornell added.

School policies on bullying need to be disentangled from concerns about school shootings and school safety, Cornell said. "Those policies need to be based on the recognized harms associated with bullying, not on the fear of school shootings," he said. Instead of thinking about security as the first line of defense against a school shooting or other serious act

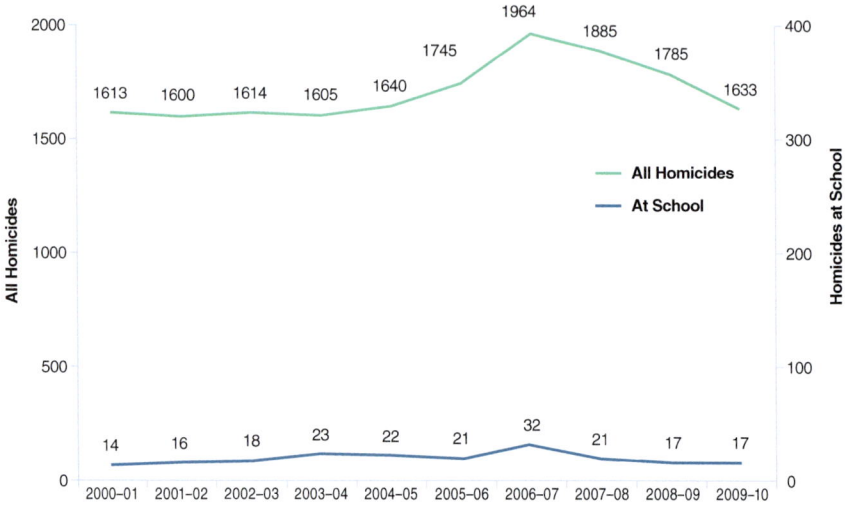

**FIGURE 4-1** Homicides at school are a tiny fraction of all homicides of youth ages 5 through 18.
SOURCE: Cornell presentation, 2014. Data from CDC, 2014a,b.

of violence, he said, the focus should be on prevention and mental health services in schools, threat assessment, and bullying prevention programs.

Almost all of the states have passed legislation related to bullying (see Chapter 9), but the legislation varies greatly from state to state, Cornell said. Usually, legislatures direct schools to come up with their own policies about bullying, sometimes with guidance to address things like defining and prohibiting bullying and mandating staff reporting for bullying, Cornell said.

Policy recommendations for schools also exist. For example, he suggested the following guidelines:

- Clarify the definition of bullying for the school community (students, staff, parents).
- Detect and intervene to stop bullying, but do not use zero tolerance.[1]
- Use valid measures to assess bullying.

---

[1] Zero tolerance refers to "a philosophy or policy that mandates the application of predetermined consequences, most often severe and punitive in nature, that are intended to be applied regardless of the gravity of behavior, mitigating circumstances, or situational context" (APA Zero Tolerance Task Force, 2008, p. 852).

- Use evidence-based strategies to reduce bullying and intervene with victims, perpetrators, and bystanders.
- Recognize when bullying is criminal or discriminatory.

School policies also face an array of challenges, Cornell said. First, state definitions of bullying tend to be very inclusive. They include almost any form of intentional peer aggression and rarely mention the power imbalances that are featured in most research definitions of bullying. As a result, he said, the more narrow definitions of bullying used in evidence-based programs tend not to line up with the definitions of bullying used in schools.

Second, students are often unwilling to report bullying, Cornell said. A more supportive school climate and change in peer culture could help with this code of silence, but schools also need more systematic and effective ways to identify victims, he said, including tip lines, peer nomination surveys, and active staff monitoring and inquiry.

Third, Cornell said, schools tend to rely on anonymous self-report surveys, but anonymous surveys cannot be validated against independent criteria. Furthermore, self-reports depend on student knowledge and understanding of the complex concept of bullying (Cornell and Cole, 2011).

Fourth, many bullying prevention programs have little or no scientific support, Cornell said, so policies need to encourage greater use of evidence-based programs. Unfortunately, he said, some legislators mistrust the idea of relying on scientific research rather than on deeply held values, and the programs most often used in schools often feature motivational speakers and 1-day programs that are of unknown effectiveness rather than programs that have been studied by researchers and have empirical support for their use.

Fifth, bullying and harassment are often confused and used interchangeably. Harassment has legal significance, whereas bullying does not, Cornell noted, and harassment does not require a power imbalance.

The U.S. Department of Education (2013) has made what Cornell called "excellent recommendations" to address the bullying of students with disabilities, which can become severe enough to deny such students a free and appropriate public education. In fact, Cornell suggested that these recommendations could apply equally well for all students. These recommendations are to:

- Use a comprehensive multi-tiered behavioral framework
- Implement clear policies on bullying
- Collect data on bullying, such as frequency, types, and location of bullying behavior, and adult and peer responses
- Notify parents or guardians of both the student who was the target of the bullying behavior and the student who engaged

in the bullying behavior of any report of bullying that directly relates to their child when bullying occurs
- Address ongoing concerns about a student's behavior that is not safe, responsible, or consistent with established school expectations through specific feedback on behavior, increased adult engagement, or more focused skills instruction
- Sustain prevention efforts

These recommendations were created partly in response to concerns about harassment and legal action, but they also reflect lawsuits in which parents in the community have successfully sued schools for victimization of their children, Cornell said.

In concluding, Cornell noted that federal protections from bullying are largely limited and piecemeal. They are concerned with bullying when it targets someone based on sex, race, color, national origin, or disability status, he said, but "all students are entitled to protection from unlawful discrimination and harassment." The overarching concern should be the protection of all children and youth from bullying, he concluded.

## DIFFERENCES BETWEEN THE UNITED STATES AND OTHER COUNTRIES

During the discussion period, an interesting exchange centered on why some bullying prevention programs are less effective in the United States than in other countries, as Bradshaw had mentioned in her presentation. U.S. schools emphasize testing and high-stakes accountability, Bradshaw observed, which puts tight constraints on how the schools can spend their time. She also pointed to cultural differences between societies in the levels of violence and exposure to violence in the media. Such differences also exist among U.S. schools, she said. For example, many bullying prevention programs have been studied in suburban communities rather than in urban settings, which may influence the effect sizes of the interventions. Students in urban communities tend not to even use the word "bullying," and they may have strong cultural norms against reporting on others, Bradshaw said.

Given this variability, adapting interventions to the particular culture is critical, Bradshaw said. "We need to work with our community partners to figure out adaptation that is strategic and appropriate," she said. "We have to make sure that we are thinking culturally and contextually about taking models not only from Europe but even within the United States. What might work in a suburban community may not work very well in inner-city Chicago or DC or Baltimore."

Gottfredson added that another possible explanation for the lesser effectiveness of bullying prevention programs in the United States is the quality of the implementation of the programs. When she and her colleagues collected information about the number of different programs that schools are implementing, she said, "we were astounded to see that the average school is implementing 17 different programs at the same time. When we looked at the quality indicators, they were very extremely low. . . . I think that is one possible reason why we see differences in the U.S."

# 5

# Family-Focused Interventions

---

**Key Points Made by Individual Speakers**

- Relatively little research has examined the role of parents and families on issues related to bullying. (Holt)
- Parents tend to report lower rates of bullying than do children, partly because children may not tell parents about bullying experiences. (Holt)
- Youth who are involved in bullying report more mental health difficulties than their parents think they are experiencing. (Holt)
- Research is investigating how factors such as family violence, poor parenting practices, hostility within families, and family dynamics that are overprotective or conflict avoidant may increase the risk of bullying involvement. (Gorman-Smith)
- Although most bullying prevention efforts are school-based, parent training and involvement are key to the prevention of bullying and victimization. (Gorman-Smith)
- Some family-based interventions that have focused on reducing violence and aggression also may decrease bullying. (Gorman-Smith)

Families and parents—including legal guardians and other caregivers—are critical influences on the health of children and adolescents, including influencing their involvement in bullying. Parent perceptions, their responses to bullying behaviors, and family-level interventions relevant to bullying are therefore major considerations in bullying prevention.

## PARENT ATTITUDES ABOUT AND RESPONSES TO BULLYING

Less is understood about parents' role in bullying issues than about the various other bullying-related factors discussed at the workshop, said Melissa Holt, an assistant professor at the Boston University School of Education. Multiple studies have found that parents tend to report lower rates of bullying than do students, she said. The discrepancies in reporting vary somewhat based on the type of bullying being assessed and on the gender of the child, she said, but youth often do not tell their parents about bullying experiences, even though parents usually think they would.

How do parents respond to bullying problems? It varies, depending on whether a child is the perpetrator or victim, Holt said. One study found that only 24 percent of children who bully said that their parents talked to them about their perpetrating behaviors, while, in sharp contrast, 62 percent of youth who were being bullied said their parents discussed those victimization experiences with them (Houndoumadi and Pateraki, 2001).

A Dutch study found that among elementary school children who said their parents knew that bullying was happening, 24 percent reported that the parents did nothing to try to stop it (Fekkes et al., 2005). Another 37 percent of the students said their parents tried to intervene, with varying levels of effectiveness; only 17 percent of the children reported that their victimization decreased as a result. However, Holt said, "when parents do become involved and provide appropriate support, often the negative effects of bullying can be diminished," including thoughts of suicide among victimized children.

Holt described two of her own studies in this area, with the caveat that they are basic research and require follow-up work. In the first project, which focused on 205 fifth graders at 22 schools and their parents, she and colleagues collected matched datasets to examine bullying perpetration and victimization; parents' attitudes, awareness, and responses to bullying; and student versus parent concordance (Holt et al., 2008). Family characteristics and functioning, including areas such as conflict, support, and monitoring, were also examined.

Consistent with previous research, youth in this study reported more bullying involvement than parents thought was occurring, Holt said. For instance, among the 16 percent of students who reported that they were being teased, only about two-thirds of the parents correctly believed their child was being teased, while the other one-third of the parents did not think their child was being victimized. That is, in 5.5 percent of the cases a child was being teased and the parent was unaware. Discrepancy rates were even higher for scenarios where children reported they were bullying other youth: "In 11 percent of the cases the child said that they perpetrate bullying behaviors, and the parent said 'No, my child doesn't,'" Holt explained. Conversely, parents sometimes reported a problem when the child did not. For example, in one-third of the cases where students said they were not being teased, their parents thought they actually were being teased.

When such mismatches in reporting occur, who should one believe? What is the reality? Holt is not sure. But as she and Gorman-Smith emphasized later in the discussion period, what matters more is the child's view of the situation, because research indicates that children's mental health outcomes are ultimately influenced by their perceptions.

Holt's study also found that about 37 percent of parents thought that schools should deal with bullying without parental interference. In addition, child maltreatment and violence in the home environments were linked to bullying involvement for both victims and perpetrators, Holt said, although only according to the self-report data from the children.

A second study by Holt and colleagues compared the views of 480 students in grades 3 to 8 and 159 of the students' parents on bullying involvement while also investigating the link to mental health (Holt et al., 2008). The study design was limited in that it did not collect matched data sets, Holt said. Again, children reported more bullying than their parents did across a range of behaviors, from teasing and spreading rumors to cyberbullying (see Figure 5-1). There was a striking discrepancy in parents' awareness of cyberbullying, perhaps because "parents are less aware of what is going on with the children online," Holt said. Furthermore, many parents of bullied children were unaware their children had missed school because of fears of being harassed. Children were more likely to talk to friends about bullying than to an adult at home, but, importantly, the youth who reached out to parents or guardians found them helpful in negotiating effective solutions, Holt said.

To assess mental health, the researchers asked the students to rate themselves on emotional function, conduct, hyperactivity, social behavior, and other areas. Across all these domains, youth who were involved in bullying "are reporting more associated mental health difficulties than parents feel their children are experiencing," Holt said (see Figure 5-2). One unfortunate implication is that parents often are "minimizing their children's experiences, which probably leads to fewer interventions and less support," she said. The broader research literature on child psychopathology makes it clear that these sorts of mismatches in reporting occur when children have behavioral and emotional problems—and that when greater discrepancies

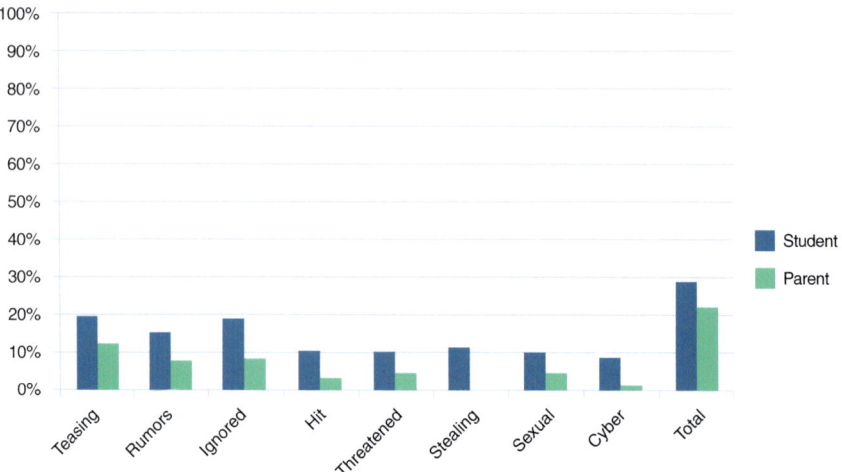

**FIGURE 5-1** Children report higher rates of bullying than do their parents.
SOURCE: Holt et al., 2008.

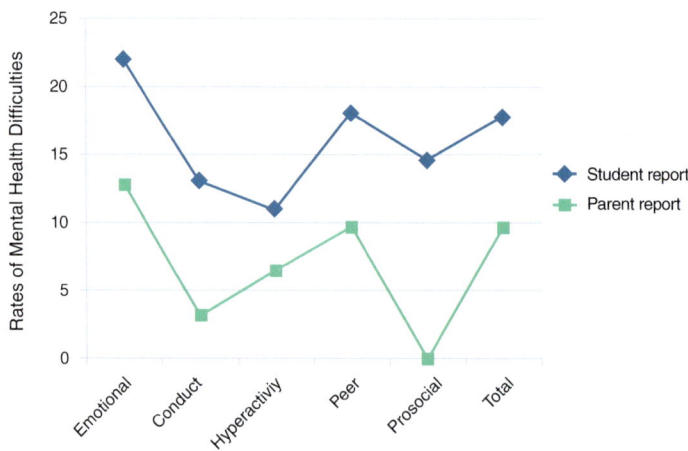

**FIGURE 5-2** Children report higher rates of mental health difficulties associated with bullying than do their parents.
SOURCE: Holt et al., 2008.

exist, children can have worse mental health outcomes. The same might apply with bullying, Holt said. "When parents don't understand what is going on for the kids, the children's mental health might be compromised."

In conclusion, Holt emphasized that experts need to encourage parents to get involved with bullying problems because their engagement is the key to prevention. She wrapped up by listing six points of advice for parents concerned about bullying, which she took from an article by Lovegrove et al. (2013):

- Maintain open communication with children
- Identify warning signs
- Coach children on responses to bullying
- Model kindness and leadership
- Work with the school
- Promote children's strengths

## FAMILIES AS SOURCES OF RISK AND PROTECTION

Deborah Gorman-Smith, professor in the School of Social Service Administration at the University of Chicago, who studies aggression and violence in children, pointed out that there currently are no family-focused intervention programs that are specifically aimed at preventing bullying. The burden of dealing with bullying has fallen upon schools, she said. Given that the developmental research literature suggests "family is one of the most important developmental influences on our behavior," she argued for an increased focus on families.

Families play three different types of roles that are relevant to bullying, Gorman-Smith said: They affect bullying risks directly (What is happening within the family that increases risk for children to perpetrate or become victims of bullying?), they influence bullying risks arising from environments outside the family (How do families help manage the contextual risks of schools or neighborhoods?), and they can act to protect children from bullying and encourage them to engage in healthy behaviors.

The relatively little research conducted so far on risks for bullying that arise from within families has looked at family violence, parenting practices, and family relationship characteristics—all factors that relate to the risks for aggression and violence more generally, Gorman-Smith said. Some research indicates that youth who live in families where there is intimate partner violence or child abuse and neglect are at significantly increased risk for engaging in bullying behavior (Smokowski and Kopasz, 2005). Other studies have examined such questionable parenting practices as harsh discipline and poor monitoring of how children spend their time and who their friends are as well as such family relationship characteristics as hostility and conflict, Gorman-Smith said. Even when families monitor and discipline their children, she added, a lack of emotional warmth and personal connection within a family "seems to be particularly important around perpetrating aggression and violence."

Much less is known about how family characteristics increase the risk of victimization. Two broad areas that seem relevant for being bullied, Gorman-Smith said, are families that are overprotective and families that tend to avoid conflict, "so that children don't have the opportunity to learn to manage conflict." However, it is difficult to disentangle cause from effect: Is a parent overprotective because the child has been victimized, or was the child more vulnerable to being victimized as a result of that parent's overprotection? (Yet another possible factor, sibling aggression, was talked about briefly during the discussion period. Both Gorman-Smith and Holt said that there is enough research to suggest that aggression between siblings may be a risk factor for bullying and victimization in the school context.)

The overwhelming majority of bullying prevention programs are school-based, and they sometimes also include parent training, which often focuses on children as victims or bystanders while, surprisingly, giving less information on the perpetration of bullying, Gorman-Smith said. In a systematic meta-analysis of school-based programs, Farrington and Ttofi (2009) found that parent training was one of the components associated with the greatest decrease in bullying and victimization. Yet training efforts for parents were often minimal, Gorman-Smith said: "They mostly consisted of informational handouts or two or three meetings where a speaker provided information about bullying. A greater focus on parenting and family might be something that could help us move the dial a bit more."

What do families need to do? Based on the larger body of research on family-focused interventions for general aggression and violence, Gorman-Smith listed a number of protective measures and goals that have been identified for working with families: nurturing parenting skills; building stable family relationships with emotional connections, clear communication, and support; encouraging the supervision and monitoring of children; increasing parental involvement in schools; and connecting families within neighborhoods with one another and to greater social support.

Many of these elements form the basis for two family-focused programs aimed at decreasing the risk for aggression and violence with which Gorman-Smith has been involved in over the past 15 to 20 years (Multisite Violence Prevention Project, 2009, 2013; Tolan et al., 2010). "We have some evidence that these probably have an impact on bullying behaviors as well," she said. One program, Schools and Families Educating (SAFE) Children, focuses on kindergarten and first-grade students. In tracking how first graders in SAFE fared when they got to high school, Gorman-Smith found a 50 percent decrease in school reports of serious misconduct including bullying, a 33 percent reduction in reports of violence, and a 20 percent increase in being "on track" for high school graduation.

The other program, GREAT Schools and Families, focuses on high-risk students in the transition from sixth grade to middle school, including students who were rated as "socially influential" (Smith et al., 2004). The researchers have observed lower reported rates of violence not only at the level of individual students participating in GREAT but also across entire schools. Other kinds of evidence-based, family-focused interventions have targeted parenting behavior, the parent–child relationship, and parental involvement in school, Gorman-Smith said.

Future research questions for exploration include the relationships between aspects of family risk and different types of bullying and victimization; ethnic, racial, and contextual differences in family risk for bullying involvement; and the developmental timing of interventions for affecting bullying behavior, Gorman-Smith said. Another question is whether existing evidence-based, family-focused interventions have had an impact on bullying; most of the well-known studies of such interventions are 20 to 30 years old and did not originally include measures of bullying behaviors, she said.

## GETTING FAMILIES INVOLVED

One topic raised during the discussion period was how to get families more engaged in bullying prevention. Even if experts had effective parenting interventions available and even if policy makers decided to implement them widely, Gorman-Smith said, "parental involvement in school has been surprisingly difficult to negotiate." One problem, she said, is that in schools in inner-city Chicago and many other places, "parents don't feel particularly welcome." Furthermore, she added, parent participation rates are typically very low for family-focused interventions.

For the SAFE Children study, Gorman-Smith and her colleagues had to expend a great deal of effort into regularly going into neighborhoods and knocking on doors. In a follow-up trial to confirm the effectiveness of their intervention, they partnered with a local community mental health agency. "Our biggest challenge was participation," she said. Most social workers at schools and staffers at community mental health agencies are trained to work with people who come in seeking services and assistance. Yet many people in the communities viewed the prevention outreach as unethical and intrusive because they were not necessarily asking for help, Gorman-Smith said. Such outreach work "really does take a personal connection with people," she added. "You can't send a flier home and expect people to come." One way that researchers have dealt with this challenge, she said, is to enlist the help of families who have benefited from the intervention project to help recruit others into the program.

One sensitive issue about research into the importance of familial factors in bullying is how the information is presented to parents, said workshop participant Deborah Temkin of the Robert F. Kennedy Center for Justice and Human Rights. "This blame element comes in," she said.

Gorman-Smith responded that it is important to clarify that familial factors may increase risks in only some cases of bullying involvement, not the majority of cases. "We are not saying this is true across the board or that parents are the sole contributors to what is going on," she said. Holt suggested framing the broader conversation around "supporting healthy and positive development" of families rather than preventing bullying or violence. The idea is that parenting is hard and that parents need more support, she said, so it is okay for them to seek ideas, information, and help from other families in managing some of these situations.

# 6

# Technology-Based Interventions

> **Key Points Made by Individual Speakers**
> - Youths use technologies for many purposes, including exploring problems; developing their identities; accessing information, resources, and support; developing networks and communities; and communicating with peers. (Mishna)
> - Cyber interventions may be a safe way for youth to access anti-bullying resources and help and to disclose incidents. (Mishna)
> - Effective interventions in non-bullying fields provide reasons for optimism that technology-based bullying prevention programs are feasible and acceptable. (Ybarra)
> - Technology-based programs require self-motivation and interest and can be costly. (Ybarra)

Bullying is an age-old behavior, noted Fred Rivara of the University of Washington School of Medicine in his opening remarks at the workshop. But the rise of social media and the increasing prevalence of technologies in children's lives may present new opportunities to ameliorate bullying.

## CYBERBULLYING AND CYBER INTERVENTIONS

In many ways cyberbullying is similar to bullying, but there are also ways in which it is not, said Faye Mishna, dean, professor, and the Margaret and Wallace McCain Family Chair in Child and Family at the University of Toronto. The cyberworld has created a new social environment for youth, she explained. Texting, e-mail, social media, chatting, social media, YouTube, apps, webcams, blogs, and other means of electronic communication are always advancing. Today's youth are increasingly immersed in technology. Ninety-nine percent have cyber access outside school, and U.S. youth spend more than 7 hours per day with digital information and communications technologies, Mishna said. Yet when stories about youth and the cyberworld appear in the media, they are often negative. These stories then tend to generate punitive laws and policies, such as zero-tolerance approaches, she said.

The important thing to recognize is that these information and communication technologies are here to stay, Mishna said. Technology may pose risks, she said, but it also can have tremendous benefits.

Young people, many of whom have never lived in a world without these technologies, use them for many purposes, Mishna said. They explore problems; develop identity; access information, resources, and support; develop networks and communities; and communicate with peers. These technologies can be especially helpful to youth lacking offline support, such as lesbian, gay, bisexual, or transgender (LGBT) youth or young people who are isolated or stigmatized, she said. "They might not be able to tell peers. They might not be able to tell school teachers. They may not be able to tell parents. [But] they may have an online world that is very supportive."

Adults may perceive youth as more technically proficient and may therefore struggle to intervene or mediate their use of information and communications technologies, Mishna said, but many youth lack the critical thinking and decision-making skills necessary for always using these technologies safely and appropriately. Often, young people make right decisions, but they sometimes slip up—and some of them slip up more than others, including those youth whom research has shown to be more vulnerable. "They need adults' input and guidance," Mishna said.

### Survey Results

Reaching young people, Mishna said, requires understanding what platforms are being used, how they are being used, and how technologies and platforms are changing. Mishna has been doing research on cyberbullying with students in grades 4, 7, and 10. Although the research is still under way, she discussed several preliminary observations and findings at the workshop.

First, the definitions and meanings associated with cyber behavior may differ considerably between adults and youth. When young people are asked whether they have been cyberbullied, they often say no, but then they describe incidents they have experienced that most adults would indeed consider cyberbullying; instead of "bullying" or "cyberbullying," the victims tend to describe these experiences by other names, such as "drama" or "trash talk." Even the idea of an aggressor and a victim in cyberbullying is often not clear, Mishna said, because the exchanges are often back and forth. Also, over time, young people have become desensitized to the kinds of things they may be pressured to do, such as sending photographs of themselves electronically to others, she said.

Furthermore, young people often do not disclose cyberbullying to adults, Mishna said. Often the only times that adults hear about cyberbullying are when something bad happens. But it is happening even when adults are unaware of it, she said. Disclosure can be very difficult, and opportunities for disclosure may be limited, Mishna said.

As part of the research ethics protocol that Mishna and her colleagues developed, they had to have a way of identifying young people who were in distress. They found that about one-quarter of the students in grades 4, 7, and 10 were in "quite serious distress," she said, which is in line with the results of surveys of mental health issues in schools and colleges. "What became very clear is that we were often the first adults they had told about it," Mishna said. Many students said they did not want to make a big deal out of their problems. They may think that telling parents and teachers will not help or else will worsen the situation. Yet by the time that young people do tell adults, the situation may indeed have become worse, Mishna observed.

### Opportunities for Intervention

Mishna provided several ideas for improving opportunities for disclosure. One is to make the disclosure mechanism highly accessible and easy for youth. Giving youth control over the process may also be important, especially in referring young people for professional help.

Cyber interventions may represent an accessible way to disclose incidents without making it a "big deal," Mishna said. However, to date, almost no research has been done on such cyber interventions, she said, and available initiatives may not be helpful, may not be comprehensive enough, or may miss the target population. As an example, Mishna cited the It Gets Better project, which emphasizes that life gets better as bullied youth grow older. But, Mishna said, this message is not necessarily helpful. First, many young people cannot wait to deal with an issue until they are adults. Furthermore, she observed, life does not get better for everyone. And, more important, some young people interpreted this message to mean that they could tell someone about a problem when such disclosures were in fact not safe. "It actually put them at risk," Mishna said. "So we have to make sure that we have online campaigns that provide tangible resources to support struggling youth at the time."

Cyber interventions may provide a safe way for youth to access resources and help, Mishna said. Because one-third of youth access health information online, it is particularly important that this information be accurate, she said. Sites designed to help youth with certain issues, such as depression, have been found to be moderately effective, with interactive sites appearing to be the most promising approach, Mishna said. In addition, research has shown that evidence-informed, school-based interventions using technology as a learning tool may be somewhat efficacious in increasing student knowledge. However, she added, these interventions tended not to change students' attitudes about cyberbullying, which is why this strategy needs to be combined with others.

Mishna closed with several recommendations for cyber interventions based on her own research. Such interventions should be continuous and not be a single event, she said, and they need to be implemented in conjunction with other strategies, including traditional therapeutic supports. Furthermore, cyber interventions need to be tailored to youth with different needs, she said, and they need to be continually adapted to youth's changing patterns of cyber use. Finally, interventions need to be made as accessible as possible in order to reduce barriers to their use. Research on the efficacy of existing interventions and how they can be improved to prevent harmful outcomes could help achieve all of these objectives, she concluded.

## INTERVENTIONS IN OTHER AREAS

Few online interventions for bullying prevention are now available, said Michele Ybarra, president and research director of the Center for Innovative Public Health Research. One of those few is Bully Text, an intervention based on text messaging that invites users to "Stand up to bullying" (DoSomething.org, 2014). Users sign up to receive messages, which walk them through a bullying scenario with the intention of creating empathy and perspective, Ybarra explained. Another campaign at the same site provides young people with examples of how to reach out to those who are being bullied in their high schools and to be a useful bystander, Ybarra said.

Ybarra also said that she was working with Dorothy Espelage (whose presentation was summarized in Chapter 3) to develop a text messaging–based bullying prevention program. Although in its infancy at the time of the workshop, it was conceived as a 6-week program, focused mostly on middle-school students, and based on a social–emotional learning framework. Students would receive three to eight messages a day for 5 weeks dealing with such topics as empathy, communication, and attitudes, with a follow-up set of booster messages. "The idea would be to have this lie on top [of what schools are doing] and make sure that young people are getting the minimum information that they need," Ybarra explained.

Ybarra spent most of her presentation talking about examples of work done with technology in non-bullying fields that have the potential to inform the development of technology-based bullying prevention programs. One such application is CyberSenga, an Internet-based HIV-prevention program for adolescents in Uganda. CyberSenga provides information, motivation, and behavioral skills related to preventing HIV infection. As Ybarra said, "Knowing that condoms are effective is one thing, but if you don't have motivation to actually use a condom, it is not that useful." The intervention was studied through a randomized controlled trial of about 360 young people, half of whom were provided with the intervention (Ybarra et al., 2013a). At 6 months post-intervention, 80 percent of those who received the intervention plus a booster intervention had not had sex in the past 3 months, compared to 57 percent of those who received just the intervention and 55 percent of those who were in the control group. Among sexually active youth, those who had sex in the past 3 months and who received the intervention plus booster were much less likely to report unprotected sex than youth in the control and intervention-only groups. These data, Ybarra said, "show that we can move the needle not just in terms of attitudes, but also in terms of self-reported behavior."

Another example was a text-messaging smoking cessation program called StopMySmoking, which was tested in Ankara, Turkey, and in the United States. It was a 6-week program based on cognitive behavioral therapy, Ybarra said. During a 2-week pre-quit period, participants received four to seven messages a day to help them reflect on why they were smoking, when they smoked, and what they could do instead of smoking. The day that they quit they received 10 messages, she said. "That whole first week is trying to be there with you in the moment." The number of messages then begins to drop, until toward the end of the period people are more independent and ready to be on their own. If people report that they did not have a cigarette, they get a reinforcing message, Ybarra said, while if they say that they slipped, they get a message about getting back on track.

In Turkey, a randomized controlled trial found that 11 percent of the people in the intervention group quit smoking, compared with only 5 percent of those in the control group, who had just received a brochure about quitting (Ybarra et al., 2012). Among light smokers, 17 percent in the intervention quit versus none in the control group, and among women,

14 percent in the intervention group quit versus none in the control group. This suggests, Ybarra said, that "no one intervention is going to be universal." In Turkey, she noted, this program seems to be well suited for women and light smokers.

In the United States, Ybarra's group looked at 150 young people between the ages of 18 and 24 who were randomly assigned either to the intervention group or to an attention-matched control group whose members received text messages at the same rate as the intervention group, but the messages were about fitness and sleep rather than about quitting smoking. Three months after the designated quit day, 40 percent of the intervention group had quit, versus 30 percent of the control group (Ybarra et al., 2013b), and the results were even better for young people who were not in college, Ybarra said.

### Online Health Information

As mentioned by Mishna, many young people look for health information online. In a national survey of more than 5,000 youth, adolescents who were bullied had significantly higher rates of seeking information online about such topics as medications, depression and suicide, drugs and alcohol, and violence and abuse (Mitchell et al., 2013). Yet the highest rates were still just 22 percent.

Online information is important, she concluded, but it should be just one tool in an overall approach to bullying prevention. Technology-based programs require self-motivation and interest, and they can be costly. Thus, Ybarra said, figuring out how to engage youth and keep them coming back may be critical.

## PREVALENCE AND RESPONSES

Two interesting subjects that arose during the discussion sessions were the prevalence of cyberbullying and the ways in which people respond to cyberbullying.

Both Ybarra and Mishna observed that cyberbullying appears to be less prevalent than is commonly assumed. Among adolescents 14 to 18 years old, cyberbullying occurs at only about one-half the rate of in-person bullying, Ybarra said, with the rates depending somewhat on the definitions and perceptions of cyberbullying. These statistics, Mishna said, "speak to the need to identify the facts and the myths that come up."

In response to a question about responses from bystanders to bullying, Mishna observed that because the cyberworld is more impersonal, bystanders have less motivation to intervene. "That is part of the education they need," she said. "While they are being witnesses, it actually can make a big difference for somebody." Ybarra pointed out that cyberbullying can seem anonymous, but usually the identity of a perpetrator is known. Still, the experience is different from standing in front of a target and a group of people.

Mishna emphasized the need for responses to be short, direct, and interactive. For example, developing an engaging way to deliver the message that bullying is hurtful could have a substantial impact, she said.

Ybarra pointed to the importance of having enough exposure to change behavior. As noted in many of the presentations, one-shot interventions do not provide enough exposure. Therefore, Ybarra said, it will be necessary to find ways to motivate young people to return to a website or other technology platform repeatedly. As Ybarra noted, building an intervention does not mean that anyone will use it. Young people need to be motivated to use a technology or communications platform, she said. Schools have a captive audience, but that is not the case online. She added that it helps if an intervention is available where youth are online, even if they are in multiple places that change over time.

In response to a question about the advisability of tracking and monitoring software to prevent cyberbullying, Mishna said that a better option would be for school districts and parents to find ways to have an interaction so that children and youth can respond to professionals online. The problem with tracking and monitoring software is that young people will find other ways to do what they want to do, Mishna said. "We want to open up the conversation and not close it." That also means providing information to adults so that they neither overreact nor minimize the problem.

In Canada, Mishna said, universities are forming taskforces with students and professors to identify the issues involving in bullying. "We have to begin that conversation, but students need to be involved," she said.

# 7

# Community-Based Interventions

---

**Key Points Made by Individual Speakers**

- Most community-based programs are not evidence-based, and evidence about programs that do work tends not be effectively communicated to practitioners. (Goldweber)
- Effective community-based programs in areas other than bullying demonstrate the potential for bullying prevention programs to exert an influence on the lives of youth. (Goldweber)
- Pediatricians and other health care professionals who work with children can advocate for bullying awareness by teachers, educational administrators, parents, and children and make the case for new laws and policies that affect bullying. (Wright)
- Pediatricians can also make valuable contributions of data to existing surveillance systems and can participate in practice-based research networks that are studying bullying and other problem behaviors. (Wright)

---

Because youths function as members of communities, community-based interventions can be a particularly effective means of reducing bullying. Yet community settings can be extremely diverse. Two presenters looked at several examples of community-based interventions, including those grounded in health care, as examples of the potential for such programs to change the norms that exist and to influence youths' experience of their communities.

## EFFECTIVE COMMUNITY-BASED PROGRAMS

Youth have a four times greater chance of being the victim of violent crime during after-school hours to when they are in school, and juvenile crime triples outside of the school setting and hours (Snyder and Sickmund, 2006). Because the after-school hours are so relatively dangerous, it is particularly important that interventions targeted at this period—i.e., community-based interventions—be effective and evidence-based, but most are not (Glasgow et al., 2003; Ringwalt et al., 2009; Saul et al., 2008; Woolf, 2008), observed Asha Goldweber, a behavioral health researcher in SRI International's Center for Education and Human Services. And, she added, information about programs that do work tend to not be effectively communicated to practitioners (Kerner and Hall, 2009; Saul et al., 2008).

A notable exception to this observation is the work of Swearer et al. (2006) on the importance of neighborhood- or community-level *collective efficacy*, which Goldweber defined as a neighborhood's connectedness and willingness to intervene with regard to youth problem behaviors (Odgers et al., 2009). Essentially, she said, this makes the entire community a bystander to bullying. An informal application of this principle, Goldweber said, is a program in Baltimore called Safe Passages, in which garbage collectors act as informal monitors as students make their way through neighborhoods. Another example is a program in California called Homeboy Industries, which was developed by a pastor for severely at-risk youth caught in a cycle of recidivism. The idea, captured in the slogan "Jobs, not jails," is to provide young adults with skills and training so that they can break the cycle of crime and delinquency, she explained.

Goldweber described a number of community-based interventions that are being evaluated using criteria evaluation developed by Blueprints for Healthy Youth Development, which is one of several sets of criteria for the evaluation of interventions. According to these criteria, for a program to be deemed "promising" it must meet a minimum standard for the specificity, quality, impact, and readiness for dissemination of an intervention. "Model programs" must meet a set of higher standards, including having been validated by a minimum of two high-quality randomized controlled trials or one high-quality randomized controlled trial and one high-quality quasi-experimental evaluation. In addition, the impact of a model program must be sustained for a minimum of 1 year after the intervention ends, Goldweber said.

Because no community-based programs that focus specifically on bullying prevention are in the evaluation phase, Goldweber discussed three other programs for which evaluations are available and which may be applicable to the development of bullying prevention programs: the Big Brothers and Big Sisters of America, the Communities That Care, and the Multidimensional Treatment Foster Care programs.

The Big Brothers and Big Sisters of America program matches adult volunteer mentors with at-risk children with the expectation that a caring and supportive relationship will develop, Goldweber explained. Multiple evaluations of the Big Brothers and Big Sisters of America program have been conducted at various locations and among a variety of demographic groups, she said, although most of these studies have been small and have lacked methodological rigor. The best study, Goldweber said, which still does meet quality standards, was conducted by Public/Private Ventures beginning in 1991 (Tierney et al., 1995). Outcomes that have been examined include a wide range of effects, including delaying initiation of substance use, academic performance, relationships with family and peers, self-concept, and social and cultural enrichment. The program has been shown to cut illicit drug initiation by 46 percent and to reduce alcohol initiation by 27 percent, although that decrease is only marginally significant. Also notable, youth reported that they were less likely to hit someone at the 1-year follow-up. There were significant reductions in truancy and cutting class and significant effects on risk and protective factors, including improvements in the quality of relationships with parents, marginally significant improvements for peer emotional support, and positive effects on schoolwork competency, Goldweber said.

Communities That Care (also described in Chapter 10) is a prevention system that gives communities the tools to address adolescent health and behavior problems through a focus on empirically identified risk and protective factors. It encompasses the five steps of getting started, getting organized, developing a community profile, creating a plan, and implementing and evaluating that plan, Goldweber said.

An evaluation of the program found reductions in self-reported violent behaviors at the 1-year follow-up (Hawkins et al., 2012), Goldweber reported. Compared with youth in the comparison group, youth under the Communities That Care program were 25 percent less likely to have initiated delinquent behavior and 32 and 33 percent less likely to have initiated alcohol and cigarette use, respectively.

Finally, the Multidimensional Treatment Foster Care program finds out-of-home placements for youth from the juvenile justice, foster care, and mental health systems, Goldweber said. According to Kerr et al. (2009), 12 months after baseline, boys in the program were incarcerated for 60 percent fewer days, had fewer subsequent arrests, and exhibited less drug use. At the same point, girls in the program had fewer days in locked settings, fewer criminal referrals, lower caregiver-reported delinquency, and more time spent on homework, Goldweber said.

## Community-Based Research

Goldweber also described community-based participatory research, which brings community members to the table shoulder-to-shoulder with interventionists and researchers. Among the many factors that affect this research, she said, are buy-in through relationship building, engaging gatekeepers, trust, communication, return on investment, capacity, sustainability, and cultural response.

An excellent example of such research, Goldweber said, is the PARTNERS youth violence prevention program (Leff et al., 2010). In this program, Leff and his colleagues meet community members in the community instead of in an academic setting, thereby reducing the perception of a power imbalance. They have informal meetings over a meal so that they can talk about what both parties' perceptions are for the goals to be achieved, and they agree to remain at the table even when disagreements arise, Goldweber said.

Another example, she said, is the Holistic Life Foundation, which is a nonprofit organization based in Baltimore, Maryland, that provides mindfulness-based interventions in an after-school setting. It trains young adults in the community to become the interventionists. "The kids who are receiving the intervention are seeing someone who looks like them and that they may already know from their community," she said. "This is changing the cultural or the community climate. It is also invoking that construct of neighborhood collective efficacy."

Goldweber said that the most important step is to get all of the stakeholders together at the table. She also emphasized the importance of meeting people where they are. Instead of having meetings at a university, practitioners and researchers can have meetings in the community or provide bus fare and meals for meeting participants.

Community-based participatory research needs to meet certain standards of effectiveness, such as the Blueprint guidelines, Goldweber said, but such programs can also balance the demands for systematic implementation of community-based interventions with being responsive to the immediate needs of the community. In addition, issues of generalizability can arise across contexts, because programs developed in one country or region may not generalize to other countries or regions. Strict monitoring of the integrity of the intervention's implementation is necessary to arrive at a scientifically successful and generalizable program, Goldweber said.

Measures of success can vary across communities. For example, Leff and his colleagues met with community stakeholders and either worked to adapt existing measures or to develop new measures that would more accurately represent the community's experience, Goldweber said. "Researchers can work with the community to develop new measures that still meet scientific standards but that are culturally responsive," she said.

Finally, Goldweber briefly described her work in California on teacher credentialing initiatives and voluntary accreditation processes for community-based organizations that are intended to ensure understanding of student mental health issues. "It is not that the teachers become student mental health providers," she said, "but that they are aware of the signs and then can appropriately refer students to the necessary stakeholders." The idea of voluntary accreditation processes for community-based organizations might start a conversation about the importance of community-based research that is also evidence based, she suggested.

## ROLES OF HEALTH CARE PROFESSIONALS

For health care professionals, the issue of bullying has largely been subsumed into the broader issue of violence, said Joseph Wright, a professor and vice chair in the Department of Pediatrics and a professor of emergency medicine and health policy at the George Washington University Schools of Medicine and Public Health. Injury due to violence is a substantial problem facing pediatricians, pediatricians feel they have an important role to play in prevention, and parents believe that pediatricians have a central role to play in prevention, according to surveys conducted by the American Academy of Pediatrics (AAP). This interest in violence prevention led the AAP in 2009 to issue a policy statement on the role of the pediatrician in youth violence prevention (Wright et al., 2009). According to Wright, this statement was focused largely on bullying as an emerging topic and one that pediatricians need to be prepared to address no matter in which setting they practice.

The question, Wright said, is, "What is a pediatrician to do?" In his answer, he focused on two kinds of approaches for pediatricians: awareness and advocacy at the community level, and anticipatory guidance at the level of clinical practice.

In the community, Wright said, pediatricians need to advocate for bullying awareness by teachers, educational administrators, parents, and children as well as for the role of health care professionals as appropriate public health messengers through print, electronic, or online media. Pediatricians see children and families repeatedly over time, so they have repeated opportunities to provide information and increase awareness. Furthermore, Wright said, pediatricians and others who see the effects of bullying behavior have many opportunities to make the case for new laws and policies.

The majority of states still do not require anti-bullying education as part of the professional development for educators, Wright said. However, the AAP policy statement recommends that pediatricians have a working familiarity with *Connected Kids*, which is the AAP's primary care violence prevention protocol. *Connected Kids* includes provisions for screening, counseling, appropriate and timely treatment, and referral for violence-related problems, including bullying (AAP, 2014).

When parents take their children to a pediatrician, they should expect the children to receive anticipatory guidance from the doctor, Wright said. The kinds of questions a pediatrician might ask of a child are:

- Have you been in any pushing or shoving fights?
- What happens when you and your friends argue or disagree?
- What do you do for fun?
- What do you like best about school?
- If you see someone being bullied, what do you do?

Such questions are child centered and parent centered, are connected to the community in which a family lives, and have a primary focus on the physical safety of children, Wright said. The questions are designed to be open ended rather than leading to a close-ended response. The emphasis is not on risk, he explained, but rather on helping the children become strong, resilient, and healthy and socially oriented.

Research has demonstrated the value of anticipatory guidance, Wright said. For example, an analysis conducted at the Harborview Injury Prevention Center at the University of Washington with preschool children found that parental cognitive stimulation and emotional support, which are provided by reading with children or having meals together, are independently and significantly protective against bullying (Zimmerman et al., 2005). This study also found that each additional hour of daily television viewing is significantly associated with the development of subsequent bullying behavior. These results are "a promising outcome for the anticipatory guidance approach," Wright said.

For middle childhood, brochures are available to both pediatricians and parents—as part of the *Connected Kids* curriculum—on independence, drug abuse, friends, anger, and bullying, Wright said. These brochures provide pediatricians with a way to address the issue of bullying in the most common health care setting that children will encounter, which is the office-based setting, he said.

Finally, Wright pointed out another valuable contribution that pediatricians can make to anti-bullying efforts: They can contribute data to existing surveillance systems. They can also participate in practice-based research networks that are studying bullying and other problem behaviors.

Wright also noted, in response to a question about opportunities presented by the Patient Protection and Affordable Care Act, that the health care profession, in the context of Medicaid expansion, is working on a uniform tool for behavioral health screening in the clinical setting. Such a tool could produce broader compliance with recommendations for early and periodic screening, diagnosis, and treatment, he said.

In response to another question, Wright observed that the universal definition of bullying enables the collection of information that could be kept in an electronic health record. More uniform reporting and responses to bullying could help school systems, health care practitioners, and other groups that interact with children, such as parks and recreation departments, speak the same language and be on the same page, he said.

## THE FOCUS OF PREVENTION

One issue that arose during the discussion session was whether prevention should be issue-specific or general. The moderator of the session, Angela Diaz of the Icahn School of Medicine at Mount Sinai, said, "The way that we do prevention tends to be very distinct and issue specific—pregnancy prevention, sexually transmitted disease prevention, HIV prevention, bullying prevention, and the funding tends to be like that also, very separate and categorical." We should consider the benefits of a more integrated prevention approach, Diaz said, because often the same youth may get involved in multiple of these behaviors or be at risk for multiple of these outcomes. In addition, having a more integrated prevention approach is likely to be more cost effective, she said.

Wright said that a universal approach to prevention has many positive aspects. For example, the project at the University of Washington, which encouraged parental cognitive stimulation and emotional support of children to deal with various potential issues, stressed primary prevention, not secondary prevention after an issue is present. Goldweber agreed that early and universal prevention approaches, such as focusing on kindness or compassion, are needed, along with funding that cuts across outcomes.

Wright agreed with a questioner that pediatricians have limited time with children and parents. But if anti-bullying interventions were incorporated as part of a longitudinal approach to prevention, he said, the time pressures would be less difficult. This approach needs to begin when children are young, he said, and then continue as they age.

Diaz also emphasized the "sacred space" of the clinic. "Young people are willing, if you ask them directly, to share their entire life with you, but it does not have to be the physician doing this questioning," she said. "We have many different members of the team—the nurses, the health educators, the social workers, and others. . . . We will know the life of the kids, their strengths and assets as well as what they struggle with, what is really in their soul. They are willing to put it out there in that type of environment. I have not necessarily seen such willingness to share in other types of environments."

# 8

# Peer-Led and Peer-Focused Programs

> **Key Points Made by Individual Speakers**
> - Bullying is not necessarily an emotional reaction but rather an attack on another youth, and it can be induced by coercion or contagion of aggressive actions by peers. (Dishion)
> - Interventions that support adult involvement, positive relationships, group management skills, and nonaggressive norms in schools can have positive effects on problem behaviors. (Dishion)
> - Individual interventions are more likely to be effective and cost beneficial than group interventions that bring together aggressive youth. (Dodge)

Much of what happens among adolescents happens away from adults, said Jonathan Todres of the Georgia State University College of Law, who moderated the session on peer-led and peer-focused programs. "They are experts, in many respects, on their lives and the lives of their peers," he said. Two speakers explored the potential of bullying prevention programs to tap into that expertise.

## PEER IMPACT ON CHILD DEVELOPMENT

Youth who exhibit behavior problems as adolescents often have traveled along a developmental trajectory in which parenting contributions and amplifying mechanisms have led to a cascading series of problems, including reactive and proactive antisocial behavior (see Figure 8-1), explained Thomas Dishion, the director of the Prevention Research Center and a professor of psychology at Arizona State University. Bullying tends to be a proactive behavior, he observed. It is not necessarily an emotional reaction, but rather a planned attack on another youth.

Two microsocial dynamic processes can amplify these problem behaviors: coercion and contagion, Dishion explained. Coercion is negative reinforcement—or escape conditioning—for peer aggression. "If I escalate and the person backs down, I am more likely to escalate and be aggressive in the future," he said. Contagion is mutual positive reinforcement for antisocial talk and behavior among peers, which also has been called deviancy training. For example, Dishion explained, in deviancy training a child might talk about something deviant, a peer laughs, the child escalates the story, and the peer further encourages the behavior. After just 30 minutes of videotaped

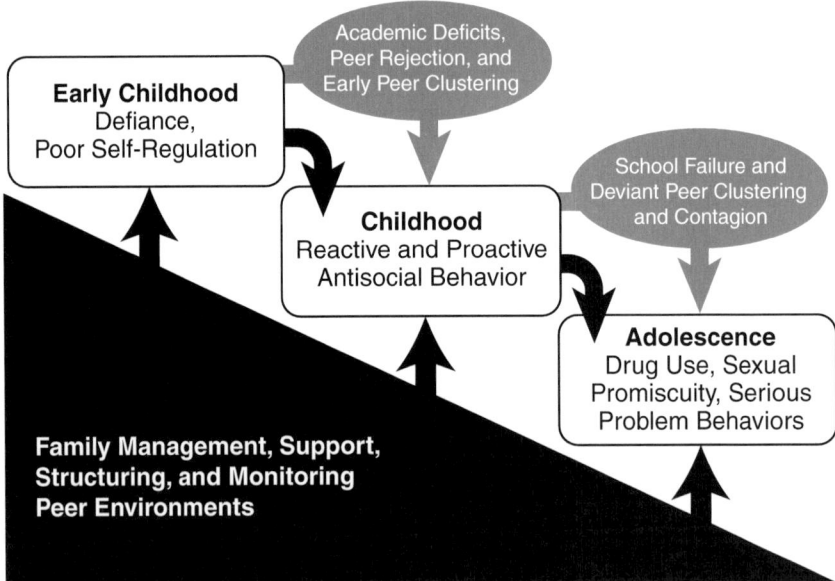

**FIGURE 8-1** Parenting contributions and amplifying mechanisms can lead to a developmental cascade of problem behaviors.
SOURCE: Dishion presentation, 2014.

observation of such conversations, children are much more likely to perform deviant acts, Dishion said. These are normal rather than pathological behaviors, he emphasized, and developmentally they can happen as early as kindergarten. "Kids will aggregate on the playground, and they will start to reward each other for these types of aggressive positions," he said. "That clustering will lead to more and more aggressive acts."

### Gang Formation

Recently, Dishion has also been looking at what he called coercive joining, where aggressive youth achieve status by forming a gang. Since at least the beginning of the 19th century, Dishion noted, gangs have existed in the United States, and they remain prevalent in many impoverished neighborhoods and cities. Several factors predict gang involvement (Dishion et al., 2005). For females, these factors include a history of antisocial behavior, a history of rejection by peers and teachers, and poor grades. For males, the same factors are involved as well as peer acceptance. "Some of the kids who we think are potentially problematic are higher social status in the peer group," Dishion said. "That might be part of the dynamic that maintains bullying and aggressive behavior."

Gang involvement is important in the progression from youths being aggressive on the playground to being dangerous in the community, Dishion said. When 16-year-olds are videotaped interacting in the laboratory, they can be seen talking about victimizing other people, whether members of the other gender or some other outgroup, he said. They escalate their aggressive behavior and can exhibit a struggle for dominance in the room. That dynamic predicts young adult dangerousness, Dishion said, including assaults, robberies, and violence. Yet the fact that it is occurring at age 16 suggests that at least some of these dynamics are malleable, he said.

In some neighborhoods, aggressors achieve more status by becoming more dangerous. For example, Djikstra et al. (2010) have shown that in some neighborhoods in New York, carrying a weapon gives youth greater status. "This is part of the issue that we need to understand," Dishion said.

### Moderating the Influence of Peers

A number of factors moderate peer influence, Dishion said. Youth with higher levels of self-regulation and lower impulsivity are less influenced, for instance, while youth with a history of peer rejection tend to be more influenced by peer norms. Some young people embrace a false consensus by perceiving that peers endorse the deviant norms. And adults who skillfully monitor or structure peer environments can reduce contagion, Dishion added. "I like to think of it as adult leadership," he said. "Having adults be in a leadership role, taking a stand, and dealing with these minor events when they are occurring and not letting them escalate is certainly a key to moderating peer influence."

Dishion also pointed to several conclusions and promising directions that emerge from this work. Interventions that support adult involvement, positive relationships, and group management skills are likely to have positive effects on problem behavior and also to reduce peer coercion and contagion, he said. Examples include the Positive Behavior Interventions and Supports program, the Good Behavior Game, and the Olweus program. Mobilizing parents in a way that puts them in a leadership role is also part of the solution, he said.

Instilling nonaggressive norms in the context of schools is likely to have positive effects, Dishion said. Norms are important, as is leadership about the kinds of norms that are guiding interactions in a school or neighborhood, he added.

Finally, more attention needs to be paid to preventing the self-organization of youth into groups that promote aggression and victimization, Dishion said, and these interventions need to start in childhood. "The development of identity around a gang is very difficult to reduce or treat once it has happened," he said. "But prevention is certainly possible, and there is some evidence to suggest that even family-based interventions can reduce the involvement of gangs in early adolescence."

## PEER INTERVENTION PROGRAMS

Kenneth Dodge, the William McDougall Professor of Public Policy and director of the Center for Child and Family Policy at Duke University, discussed two approaches to the prevention of bullying. The first is to build social competencies within the aggressor. This can be done one-on-one with an adult trainer and the individual child, it can be done in groups in which the bullying child is interacting with non-aggressive peers, or it can be done in groups of other aggressors, Dodge said.

The techniques to help a child build social skills that will help that child refrain from bullying and aggression have improved dramatically in recent decades (Dodge and Sherrill, 2006). Interventions that have proven effective include cognitive behavioral therapies, cognitive behavioral skills building, social skills building, and social problem-solving training, Dodge said.

However, most policies are not directed toward individual skill building, Dodge said. Instead, the most common way to deal with an aggressive or deviant child is to place that child with other deviant peers in systematic interventions. For example, group therapies or milieu therapies are common in mental health and account for more than one-half of the expenditures in the mental health arena for aggressive behavior, Dodge said. In the area of education, he noted, a variety of interventions—tracking, special education, in-school suspensions, and alternative schools—place children with similar issues together. And the juvenile justice system places delinquents in training schools and boot camps and incarcerates them, with group-based interventions accounting for more than 90 percent of juvenile justice expenditures, Dodge said. "It is our most common public policy for dealing with aggression and bullying," he said.

Among the rationales for peer group interventions are that they are less costly, they afford role playing and practice, they enable manipulation of peer group reinforcement, and they help youth feel comfortable, Dodge said. However, Lipsey (2006) found that, on average, group interventions are one-third less effective than individual interventions. Furthermore, many group interventions yield net adverse effects. About 42 percent of the prevention programs that Lipsey studied yielded net adverse effects, as did 22 percent of the probation programs in that study. As a result, Lipsey concluded that individual interventions are more effective and cost beneficial, Dodge said.

This conclusion, which was based on a comparison of different interventions, was supported by an experimental test using an intervention called Coping Power, which is a social-cognitive skill building intervention for 8- to 14-year-old aggressive children. The experiment compared the effectiveness of the intervention administered to individuals versus the intervention administered to groups, Dodge explained. In the study of 360 aggressive fourth-grade children in 20 different schools who were randomly assigned at the school level to receive Coping Power either individually or in deviant-only groups, the findings were somewhat mixed immediately after treatment (Lochman et al., 2013). There was some tendency for homogenization, with the most aggressive children becoming less aggressive and the least aggressive children becoming more aggressive. However, at the 1-year follow-up, the children who received the individualized intervention had much greater reductions in externalizing and internalizing problems than did the children who received the group intervention.

For situations where it is not possible to administer the intervention individually, Dodge said, strategies exist to mitigate the iatrogenic effects—that is, the negative effects on individuals caused by the treatment itself—from being part of deviant peer groups. Strong training for experienced adult group leaders, the use of behavioral reinforcement strategies, teaching strategies that emphasize clear instructions, and emphasizing a peer-culture norm of non-deviance can all reduce the negative influences of peers, Dodge said. Other approaches are to limit unstructured time with peers, to monitor hot spots where peers congregate, to limit the interaction opportunities of the peer group members by mixing children from different schools or communities, and using short-duration interventions, he said.

## Changing the Peer Culture

The second approach Dodge discussed was working with the peer environment and culture to reduce the reinforcement of bullying. Two promising approaches are the Positive Behavior Intervention and Supports (PBIS) program (Waasdorp et al., 2012) and the Supporting Early Adolescent Learning and Social Success (SEALS) model (Farmer et al., 2013).

SEALS is a teacher-training and directed-consultation model that helps teachers with managing social dynamics, enhancing academic engagement, and improving classroom behavior management, Dodge explained. In a trial in 28 middle schools randomly assigned to receive either the SEALS teacher training intervention or a control, teachers trained in the SEALS intervention were more accurate at understanding peer affiliations and became better managers of the classroom (Farmer et al., 2013). Their students made greater academic achievement gains and reported valuing school more and feeling a greater sense of belonging in the school. Students also perceived a more supportive school and peer context and interacted more with more normative peers rather than just academic peers. The researchers have not yet reported whether the intervention reduced bullying or aggression, Dodge said.

## Research Conclusions

Dodge provided four conclusions that he drew from his review of the research. First, programs, placements, and treatments that bring deviant peers together should be avoided whenever possible, he said. Such strategies include training schools, boot camps, Scared Straight, Guided Group Interaction, the Gang Resistance Education and Training Program, midnight basketball, hangouts, non-structured after-school programs, and long prison terms mandated by three strikes laws. Highly structured after-school programs may be effective, he said, depending on who is in those groups.

His second conclusion was that effective alternatives to deviant peer-group placement should be encouraged. Examples of such alternatives include individual therapies such as functional family therapy, multisystemic therapy, and multidimensional treatment foster care; therapeutic courts; early prevention programs such as the High/Scope Perry Preschool, and Fast Track; programs that combine high-risk and low-risk youths such as 4-H, school-based extracurricular activities, boys and girls clubs, scouting, and church activities; and universal peer-culture interventions like PBIS and SEALS. For older youth, Job Corps, individual skills training, and efforts to disperse rather than increase gang cohesiveness are good approaches, Dodge said.

When placement with peers is inevitable, specific measures should be implemented to minimize its impact, Dodge said. Highly susceptible youths, such as slightly delinquent early adolescents, should not be placed with deviant youths, and deviant youths with older, more deviant peers or peers with similar problems from the same community should not be combined. Experienced leaders are needed and should have training, Dodge said, and youths need to be placed in highly structured environments with little free time. It is possible to reduce problems by monitoring youths' behavior closely and keeping their placements short, he said.

Finally, practitioners, programs, and policy makers should document placements and evaluate the impacts of those placements, Dodge said. The record needs to include a description of the placement environment and of peers, he added.

## Structuring School Systems and Classrooms

One interesting application of engineering a positive peer culture, which came up in the discussion session, involved the structure of middle schools. Sixth graders who go to an elementary school have less drug use, fewer school suspensions, less deviant behavior, and higher academic test scores than sixth graders who spend their time with seventh and eighth graders, Dodge said. And, most important, those effects hold not only while the children are in sixth grade but into high school. "There is something about the way we engineer schools that we might rethink," he said.

During the discussion period, Dodge also addressed the issue of the extent to which adverse peer influences can be offset by positive peer influences. "Imagine you are the superintendent of a school system," he said. "Twenty percent of your children are deviant. Where do you place them? Are you going to have a net overall positive effect by sending them off to an alternative school or tracking them, even though it might have a negative effect on them? Is it going to have a positive effect on the other 80 percent who do not have to deal with them? After all, these placements are directed by parents of the non-deviant kids who do not want deviant kids with their well-behaving child." Dodge has been involved in research that has indicated the existence of a critical mass effect. If a class includes no more than three elementary or early middle-school children who were suspended in the previous year, he said, then those children typically have a minimal impact on their classmates. But once the number exceeds a critical mass, the deviant peer influence seems to outweigh the positive peer influence. "There may be ways to engineer the whole system to maximize the positive influence and minimize the deviant peer influence," Dodge said.

## YOUTH LEADERS

Another topic that arose during the discussion period was the influence of youth leaders on their peers. Group interactions, Dishion said, can have many effects, some positive and some negative. Youth who have turned their lives around can be especially effective leaders, but they also can have relapses and continued problems. "There is a danger there as well," he said. "You cannot emphasize enough structuring these environments so that you really have a handle on them."

Dodge pointed to empirical evidence that aggressive children are, by and large, disliked by the larger peer group in kindergarten, first grade, and second grade, but by middle school the aggressive child is more popular, at least in some contexts. In this case, he said, "one might think about how to get those deviant peer-group leaders who have influence to use their influence in a positive way rather than a negative way."

Dishion also reminded the workshop participants of the success demonstrated by programs such as Big Brothers and Big Sisters of America (see Chapter 7), which provide children and adolescents with positive role models.

On the topic of peer leaders, Catherine Bradshaw of the University of Virginia Curry School of Education noted another sort of challenge—that the youth who are volunteering for leadership roles may not be particularly influential in their peer groups. Sometimes they have a history of victimization or are from a marginalized group, she said, although they can achieve more status as they get older.

# 9

# Laws and Public Policies

---

**Key Points Made by Individual Speakers**

- As of 2014, 49 states and the District of Columbia have enacted anti-bullying laws, whose key components range widely. But little is known about the extent to which the laws and their implementation actually decrease bullying behaviors. (Hatzenbuehler)
- One Oregon study suggests that "inclusive" anti-bullying policies—those that specifically include sexual orientation as a protected-class status—reduce the risk of suicide attempts and peer victimization in gay teenagers. (Hatzenbuehler)
- Student-on-student bullying victimization can be perceived as imposing a learning disability on the targeted children because victimization creates barriers to their education. (Abrams)
- Schools face strong disincentives against enforcing state-mandated anti-bullying laws, including the risk of costly lawsuits brought by bullies and their parents claiming infringement of First Amendment speech rights. But, unlike speech, physical assaults and true threats are not protected under the law. (Abrams)
- Existing law puts school districts in a strong legal position to impose discipline in student-on-student bullying cases, but districts seeking to protect targeted students must defend lawsuits that might arise. (Abrams)

As student-on-student bullying has received greater attention in recent years, state legislatures have responded. Forty-nine states and the District of Columbia now have laws against bullying. Evaluation is critical for understanding a law's impact, how it ends up being enforced, and any unintended consequences of enforcement. Two speakers provided an overview of anti-bullying laws and policies, including how attempts to prohibit bullying fit within a broader legal framework that addresses children's issues.

## MANY ANTI-BULLYING LAWS EXIST, BUT ARE THEY EFFECTIVE?

The United States has seen a rapid proliferation of anti-bullying laws, with state legislatures enacting or amending more than 120 bills on bullying and related behaviors between 1999 and 2010. As of 2014, 49 out of 50 states have laws to prevent bullying, said Mark Hatzenbuehler, assistant professor of sociomedical sciences at Columbia University's Mailman School of Public Health. The lone exception is Montana, which does, however, have an anti-bullying policy, he said.

Scholars have developed conceptual frameworks for understanding the content and scope of laws and policies that target bullying behaviors (Limber and Small, 2003; Srabstein et al., 2008; U.S. Department of Education, 2011). In a 2011 report, the U.S. Department of Education developed a comprehensive framework to evaluate anti-bullying laws and policies in 46 states. The report identified 16 key components found in the existing laws, such as a definition of what bullying is; a list or "enumeration" of the specific groups of individuals to be protected from bullying; and requirements for communicating the law or policy to school administrators, teachers, and students. Some key components were more common than others. For example, 43 states included descriptions of bullying behaviors that are prohibited, but only 17 states enumerated protected groups. About one-third of states included at least 13 to 16 of the components, noted Hatzenbuehler.

The vast majority of research on anti-bullying legislation has focused on legal content analyses, Hatzenbuehler said, but "we know very little about the extent to which these policies are actually effective in meeting their stated goal." He and Katherine Keyes of Columbia University conducted one of the first empirical studies to look at the effectiveness of these policies (Hatzenbuehler and Keyes, 2013). They investigated whether having an "inclusive" anti-bullying policy—one that specifically includes sexual orientation as a protected class—reduced suicide risk and peer victimization (being aggressively targeted by other children) in lesbian and gay youth. Focusing on 34 counties in Oregon that had anti-bullying policies, the researchers examined 197 school districts to determine whether those policies at the district level included sexual orientation as a protected-class status. In only 15 percent of the Oregon counties did all their school districts have inclusive anti-bullying policies, Hatzenbuehler said.

The researchers linked these findings on anti-bullying policies to health and sexual orientation data collected through an annual survey of 11th-grade public school students in Oregon, including 301 lesbian and gay youth. Counties were divided into three categories ranging from "least inclusive" to "most inclusive" based on the proportion of their school districts with anti-bullying policies that included sexual orientation. Results showed that around 31 percent of lesbian and gay youth living in the least inclusive counties had attempted suicide in the past year—twice as many as the 16 percent of gay and lesbian teens who attempted suicide in the most inclusive counties (see Figure 9-1). "We find that policies that do not include sexual orientation as a protected class are not protective of lesbian and gay youth in terms of reducing the risk of suicide attempts," Hatzenbuehler said. Inclusive anti-bullying policies were also associated with a reduced risk for peer victimization for all youth, not just gay and lesbian youth.

Hatzenbuehler noted that research on the effect of anti-bullying policies is consistent with other studies that document the impact that public policies have on health and behavioral outcomes (Hatzenbuehler et al., 2009, 2010, 2012). Hatzenbuehler suggested that this is noteworthy in that it offers precedence for considering laws and public policies as one of a number of effective strategies that can be used to improve the health and well-being of young people. However, much more research is needed to study the actual effectiveness of policies in reducing bullying behaviors to establish

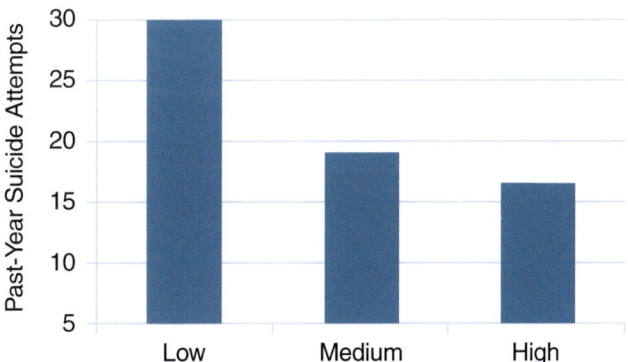

FIGURE 9-1 Counties in Oregon with more inclusive anti-bullying policies have the lowest risk of suicide attempts among lesbian and gay youths.
SOURCE: Hatzenbuehler and Keyes, 2013.

best practices for policy makers and school administrators, Hatzenbuehler said, including stronger methodologies for establishing cause-and-effect linkages. It is often unethical to conduct randomized controlled trials that would assign individuals to live in environments with or without an anti-bullying policy, he noted, but longitudinal and quasi-experimental studies can be used instead. Researchers can also take advantage of the heterogeneity in anti-bullying laws to see whether states with the more comprehensive policies have more success in reducing bullying.

If anti-bullying policies are in fact protective, Hatzenbuehler added, then experts should be studying why they work (by examining mediating factors) and for which groups of people they are most effective (by testing moderators). For example, reducing peer victimization appeared to be one of the mediating factors in Hatzenbuehler and Keyes' study. More studies are also necessary to understand the effects of putting anti-bullying laws into practice on the ground, he said. Qualitative and ethnographic studies in schools with administrators, teachers, parents, and youth could help identify barriers and facilitators in implementation, he added.

To start to address some of these critical gaps, Marizen Ramirez of the University of Iowa is conducting a longitudinal study to evaluate the implementation and outcomes of anti-bullying legislation in her state. Hatzenbuehler and Ramirez are also analyzing the legal content of anti-bullying legislation in several key U.S. regions and linking those findings to Youth Risk Behavior Surveillance data to see whether stronger laws against bullying are more effective in reducing bullying behaviors.

## HOW THE LAW BOTH HELPS AND HINDERS THE PROTECTION OF CHILDREN FROM BULLYING

To further describe the legal framework for anti-bullying regulations, Douglas E. Abrams, a professor at the University of Missouri School of Law, discussed the private and public system that protects children. The pediatric safety system has parents at the top of the hierarchy and works its way down through the public schools, law enforcement, juvenile and family courts, and state mental health agencies (Abrams, 2009). Abrams focused his remarks primarily on the public school system, because, he said, most aggressors know their victims through attending school and do not foresee that anyone but classmates will pay much attention.

Abrams highlighted the three P's of school anti-bullying efforts: perceptions, prevention, and potential legal constraints. Public policy often depends on perceptions, he said. Bullying victimization can be perceived as imposing a learning disability on child victims, he said, because it creates barriers to education similar to those identified by the Individuals with Disabilities Education Act (IDEA) (Abrams, 2012, 2013). "Bullying victimization jeopardizes the state's obligation to provide a free public education to all children," he added. The IDEA recognizes disabilities that arise from external circumstances that are very similar to bullying victimization: "Students cannot learn effectively when they are scared stiff in school," Abrams said. Such a perception of bullying's effects could motivate legislatures to act effectively; even though 49 states have anti-bullying laws, amendments are still necessary to ensure that policies work effectively, he said.

## Legal Constraints

Turning to potential constraints, Abrams cautioned that when it comes to bullying, "we need to be wary of legal solutions, which are often not useful solutions at all." States cannot prosecute, adjudicate, or discipline their way out of the bullying problem, he said, because "there is just too much bullying going on." Prosecution and juvenile court adjudication are reactive measures invoked only after somebody is already hurt. Public authorities serve children best when they can modify behavior in a preventive mode without turning to formal processes except in the most serious cases, he said.

Abrams offered three conclusions on potential legal constraints. First, he said, "the law can sometimes present major challenges to protecting bullied children." Schools may face strong professional and financial disincentives against enforcing state anti-bullying laws. Second, when bully perpetrators or their parents file lawsuits, they typically assert constitutional rights or other legal rights. Third, existing law puts school districts in a potentially strong position if they present a good case on the facts in student-on-student bullying cases, he said, but lawsuits will occur and victory is not assured.

All enforcement of state anti-bullying laws is ultimately local and depends on teachers, administrators, and others in the school building, Abrams explained. For one thing, statewide anti-bullying laws are almost always unfunded mandates, he said, so the question becomes, Who pays for implementation and enforcement? To conform with state anti-bullying laws, cash-strapped school districts have to pay to hire and train faculty, Abrams said, but he added that he nonetheless thinks that such endeavors can be cost effective. The greatest cost that school districts must bear related to anti-bullying efforts is defending against the litigation that can arise in reaction to those efforts, he said. It is not always easy for courts to determine who did what to whom, which means that judges tend to have a great deal of discretion in deciding such lawsuits. As a result, Abrams said, teachers and administrators may find that "sometimes the path of least resistance is to turn their backs on student misconduct."

Concerning the legal authority to implement anti-bullying efforts, Abrams said that public schools are in a potentially strong position. In the court's eyes, he said, schools are "special places" when it comes to discipline: The constitutional rights of elementary and secondary students inside public schools are less than their constitutional rights outside school because courts must weigh the need to protect students in school.

The seminal decision regarding students' constitutional rights in school, Abrams said, was from the 1969 case *Tinker v. Des Moines Independent Community School District* in which the plaintiffs wore black armbands to school to protest the Vietnam War. The Supreme Court held that a school may discipline students for speech that "materially or substantially disrupts school activities" or that creates a "collision with the rights of other students to be secure and to be let alone," Abrams explained. Another relevant decision, *Bethel School District v. Fraser* in 1986, involved a high school student who delivered a lewd speech in a school assembly program and later filed suit claiming that his resulting suspension violated his First Amendment speech rights. The Supreme Court held, Abrams said, that schools may regulate student speech to teach "the shared values of a civilized social order" and fundamental values, which include consideration of "the sensibilities of fellow students" and "the boundaries of socially appropriate behavior."

Many cases of bullying, including cyberbullying, also involve physical assaults, Abrams noted, and these are not protected under the law. The First Amendment does not protect true threats of violence, even verbal ones. Assaults, Abrams explained, may include pushing, shoving, spitting, and throwing a pencil at someone.

Anti-bullying legislation cannot protect school districts from lawsuits, Abrams said, but schools can prevail if they present the right kind of evidence. He emphasized that anti-bullying legislation and policies are not particularly valuable if schools are reluctant to exercise their disciplinary authority. School districts must be willing to fight lawsuits to protect students, he said.

Although 49 states have anti-bullying laws, some legislatures still have much work to do in the arena of cyberbullying, Abrams said. Most states require school districts to have policies banning cyberbullying, for example, but these statutes typically apply only to discipline imposed for what a child does in the school building, on school grounds, or on a school bus or school-sponsored trip. However, Abrams said, almost all cyberbullying is done off campus. Still, many perpetrators of cyberbullying eventually end up committing physical assaults, so schools may discipline them for those actions, he said.

## LEGAL RESPONSES TO BULLYING

During the discussion period, one questioner asked how attorneys can work with schools to encourage the implementation of new anti-bullying policies. Abrams suggested that lawyers can assure that procedures for handling bullying situations meet constitutional and nonconstitutional guidelines and that administrators carefully document their actions against bully perpetrators. In addition, he said that while school districts generally tend to lose many student free-speech cases outside the bullying area, courts do not actually require much evidence to establish that a disruption in school has been material and substantial. "If two students fight or assault one another in a classroom, that is Tinker-type disruption, which ought to win for the school district if the perpetrator can be identified," he said. If lawyers put on a good case, showing how much time teachers and schools spend dealing with animosities arising from bullying and how hurtful bullying is to students, he said, "I think the judges would be receptive." However, he added, school districts often fail to put on a proper case.

Jonathan Todres of Georgia State University College of Law asked if it is possible to address social harms such as bullying in ways that incentivize positive behavior rather than just punish bad behavior. Hatzenbuehler replied that anti-bullying policies that enumerate specific protected groups encourage better behavior by fostering more diverse, inclusive environments in schools. Researchers do not have a good handle on which types of policies—punitive versus positive reinforcement—are better at deterring bullying; that is an empirical question that needs examination, he said.

Dorothy Espelage of the University of Illinois, Urbana-Champaign, asked the speakers what advice they could give for parents who call in saying that their child is being chronically victimized, beyond telling them to document everything carefully or to move their child out of the school? Espelage noted that in a number of cases where bullied children committed suicide, parents sued school districts and lost; the districts had hired psychologists who testified that the child's suicide was due to having depression and not due to any harassment by bullies or negligence by the schools.

Abrams replied that it is hard to know what to tell parents, especially because it is not always clear to school administrators and teachers what the appropriate remedy is in a particular case. Parents may have to choose from among some bad alternatives to try to make a victimized child's life better, Abrams said. Hatzenbuehler added that judges in some cases involving lesbian, gay, bisexual, and transgender youth have been open to hearing social science research data on how bullying can affect these teens. Abrams also noted that federal civil rights statutes might apply if the bullying victim was targeted because of religion, race or ethnicity, or sexual orientation.

# Part III

# Future Directions and Overall Themes

# 10

# Translating Bullying Research into Policy and Practice

---

**Key Points Made by Individual Speakers**

- The adoption, implementation, sustainability, and scalability of an intervention receive much less study than efficacy, yet these are the factors that will determine whether an evidence-based intervention has a large-scale impact on a population. (Rohrbach)
- Even when implementing an evidence-based program, the fidelity of implementation varies greatly. (Rohrbach)
- Interventions designed to achieve multiple outcomes can produce both immediate and long-term positive outcomes, but monitoring and feedback to practitioners are needed to ensure fidelity of implementation. (Fagan)

---

As Denise Gottfredson, University of Maryland, said in introducing the panel on translating bullying research into policy and practice, developing effective interventions is just the first step in achieving high-quality implementation of effective practices on a large enough scale that they can make a substantial difference. Research on efficacy needs to be translated into effective policies and practices, as the three presenters on the panel observed. Although their talks were not necessarily specific to bullying prevention, by drawing more broadly from what has been learned about sustainability and high-quality implementation of prevention practices in general, their observations can be applied to bullying prevention.

## IMPLEMENTATION OF PREVENTION PROGRAMS IN SCHOOLS

Research on interventions has a characteristic lifecycle (see Figure 10-1), noted Luanne Rohrbach, associate professor of preventive medicine and director of the Master of Public Health program at the University of Southern California Keck School of Medicine. The initial stages of this lifecycle—pre-intervention studies, efficacy studies, and effectiveness studies—tend to receive considerable resources and emphasis, she said, while studies of the adoption, implementation, sustainability, and scalability of an intervention tend to receive much less attention. Yet, she said, these latter factors are the ones that will determine whether an evidence-based intervention has a large-scale impact on a population.

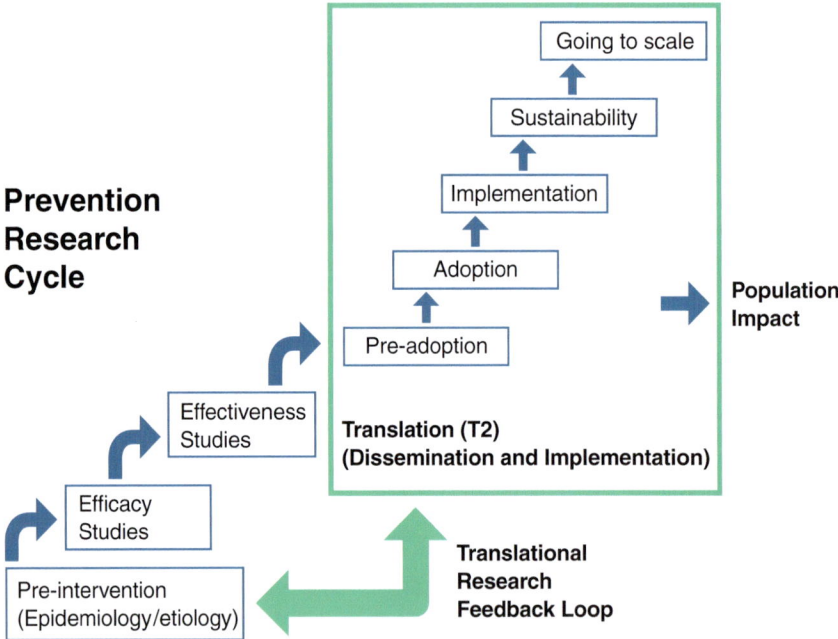

**FIGURE 10-1** Prevention research tends to focus on efficacy and effectiveness, but dissemination and implementation are the steps that have the greatest impact on populations.
SOURCE: Rohrbach presentation, 2014. Data from NRC and IOM, 2009, and Spoth et al., 2013.

Efficacy has been established for an increasing number of empirically validated prevention interventions, Rohrbach said, but less is known about the effectiveness of these interventions when implemented under real-world conditions. In addition, reviews of evidence-based programs are available, best-practice guidelines have been published, and local communities are encouraged to implement only these "proven programs," yet a gap persists, she said, between the development and testing of interventions and the implementation of those interventions.

As an example of this gap, Rohrbach briefly described a study by Ringwalt et al. (2009) that asked middle schools about their use of evidence-based programs for substance use prevention. The percentage of the schools that reported using an evidence-based program grew from less than 35 percent in 1999 to about 42 percent in 2005, but a greater increase had been expected over that period because of the implementation of a new policy that gave schools guidance in using proven programs when applying for funds for substance use prevention programs.

### Challenges in Implementing Prevention Programs

As discussed by previous presenters, schools face many challenges in implementing prevention programs, including a focus on academic achievement, limited time and resources, school reform measures, staff turnover, and a limited capability to monitor implementation and collect outcome data. Schools also have complex decision-making processes that are used to determine which interventions will be implemented and how, Rohrbach said, and the decisions have stakeholders at many levels. Furthermore, many schools have inadequate access to tools for decision making about prevention. Finally, Rohrbach said, schools have inequitable resources and limited funding for sustained prevention efforts.

Rohrbach and other researchers have examined the factors that influence the adoption and use of evidence-based programs in schools, and those factors can be divided into three categories, Rohrbach said: program-related factors, organizational factors, and the characteristics of implementers (Rohrbach and Dyal, in press; Rohrbach et al., 2006).

The first category, she said, includes factors related to the program itself. Is it attractive and user-friendly, easy to use, and flexible? Are the methods familiar? Do they offer a perceived advantage over current practice? Does a program fit with an organization's goals and work practices?

The second category includes organizational factors, including leadership, administrative support, the presence of program champions, a positive school climate, organizational norms, effective communication, openness to change, and existing capacity, Rohrbach said.

The third category includes the characteristics of the implementer. Those who are motivated, have a positive attitude toward the program, are comfortable with the approach, have the skills to implement the program, and have a strong sense of self-efficacy are more likely to adopt and implement a new evidence-based prevention program than those without those characteristics, Rohrbach said.

Several frameworks have been published that bring these categories together, Rohrbach said. One such framework includes barriers and facilitators at multiple levels of influence (see Figure 10-2). Complex interactions occur among the factors at the various levels that influence whether the implementation will be effective, Rohrbach said. The framework also emphasizes the importance of infrastructure and the capacity for prevention program delivery, she noted. For example, the training of implementers and other school personnel is extremely important. It can result in greater self-efficacy and confidence, a higher level of skill, more motivation, and more positive attitudes toward the program. There is clear evidence that training is associated with stronger implementation fidelity. Some evidence

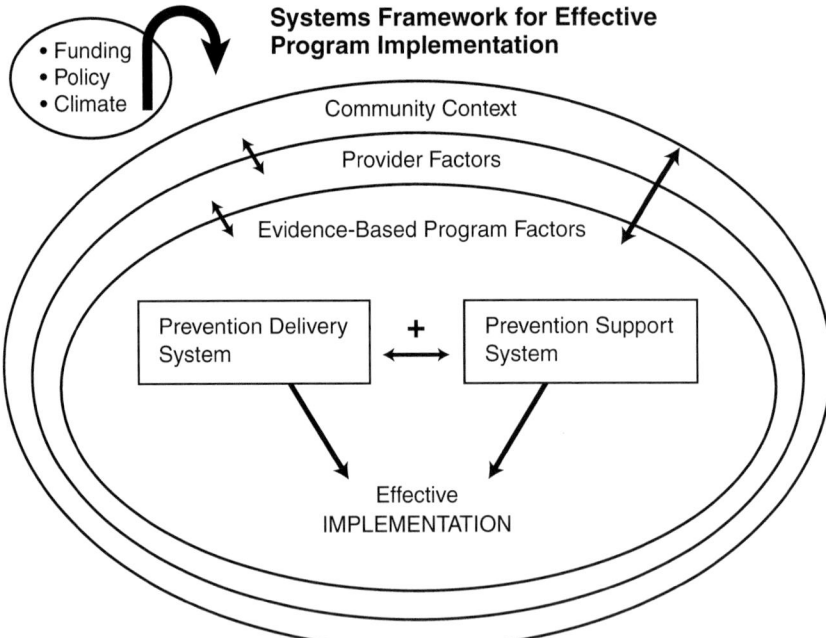

**FIGURE 10-2** Effective implementation is a product of multiple interactions among programs, providers, and the community.
SOURCE: Rohrbach presentation, 2014. Data from Durlak and DuPre, 2008.

also suggests that ongoing training, or technical assistance, enhances implementation, Rohrbach said.

Organizational capacity, which is part of the delivery system, includes resources (e.g., funds and staffing), managerial and administrative support, effective partnerships with other organizations, and data systems for continuous quality improvement, Rohrbach said. All of these factors increase the chances that a program will be implemented effectively and in a way that faithfully reflects the intentions of the program's developers, she said.

### Implementing Interventions with Fidelity

Fidelity to the intentions of a program can be measured in several ways, Rohrbach said, and adherence, dosage, and engagement are all important factors to consider. Fidelity varies greatly in school settings, she said. Some schools implement interventions with high fidelity, while others do so with much less fidelity. Teachers have reported eliminating key modules, not using interactive materials, and otherwise deviating from the program as written, she said, and combining lessons from more than one program is a common practice.

Many studies have demonstrated that fidelity is important and is associated with outcomes. As an example, Rohrbach cited the Adolescent Alcohol Prevention Trial from the 1990s (Rohrbach et al., 1993). The degree of fidelity to which the program was implemented had a substantial impact on program acceptance, substance use attitudes, program-specific knowledge, behavioral intentions, and resistance skills, she said, with high-fidelity implementations being associated with more positive outcomes.

Despite such findings, the tension between fidelity and adaptation persists, Rohrbach said. Unintentionally and intentionally, implementers modify programs in various ways in order to increase their cultural relevance, address participants' cognitive-information processing and motivation, and improve the fit between program and context, she said. It is also the case that more flexible programs are more likely to be implemented and sustained. However, little is known about the effects of adaptation on outcomes, she said, and some evidence indicates that it can result in poorer outcomes.

Guided or planned adaptation can overcome some of these problems, Rohrbach said. Ideally, the process of guided adaptation involves an interaction with the program developer. It needs to be theory based, to provide options within or among program components, to conceptualize a program as a process rather than a standardized set of activities, and to develop and adhere to guidelines for cultural adaptations, Rohrbach said.

### Implications for Practice and Research

Rohrbach concluded by providing several implications that her observations have for practice. Implementers should

- Conduct readiness assessments
- Develop a broad base of supporters for programs and involve stakeholders in planning
- Establish leadership
- Implement strategies to build capacity
- Integrate prevention programs with the school's primary mission (learning) and ongoing prevention delivery systems in the community
- Develop systems for collecting data that will guide implementation and continuous quality improvement
- Develop better systems of information about what is available and how it might fit locally
- Increase the understanding of what program implementation involves

She also listed several implications for researchers. They should

- Develop assessments of prevention program outcomes that can easily be used by schools as part of their accountability process
- Evaluate the implementation of evidence-based programs under real-world conditions
- Investigate how varying models of training and technical assistance affect implementation and student outcomes
- Ground programming in the realities of the school setting
- Conduct more cost–benefit analyses
- Investigate the effects of adaptations
- Conduct research on how evidence-based programs work to identify key ingredients

## THE COMMUNITIES THAT CARE SYSTEM

Communities That Care is a prevention system rather than a program, explained Abigail Fagan, an associate professor at the University of Florida. It is designed to build the capacity of communities to do evidence-based prevention regardless of the behaviors being prevented or promoted, and it is a community-driven approach that takes into account the differences among communities and the problems they are facing. "A one-size-fits-all approach may not be the best model," she said. "We want something that can be community specific." For example, communities differ in levels of youth delinquency, levels of risk and protective factors related to delinquency, resources, capacity, norms, and values, and, as noted in Chapter 7, youth behavior is affected by the community context.

Communities That Care emphasizes a comprehensive and coordinated approach to prevention, Fagan said. It relies on local practitioners and stakeholders to take ownership for what they want to see change in their community and then to work together collaboratively to get there. It is driven by the use of science to assess the needs and behaviors in a community, to match those needs with evidence-based practices, and to make sure that those new practices are implemented with fidelity so that they can achieve their intended outcomes, she said.

The system has five phases, which Fagan reviewed in the context of a randomized controlled study that tested the effectiveness of Communities That Care in reducing delinquency, substance use, violence, and other problem behaviors (Hawkins et al., 2014). Twenty-four communities located in small to medium-size towns in seven states were randomly assigned to carry out either the Communities That Care approach or prevention as usual, and key leaders came together in the getting-started phase to create a coalition of stakeholders. The organizations represented by community board leaders in the 12 communities participating in Communities That Care represented businesses, citizen advocacy organizations, community coalitions, health agencies, human service agencies, the juvenile justice system, law enforcement, local philanthropies, the media, parents, religious groups, schools, substance abuse prevention organizations, local governments, youth, and youth recreation programs. Communities That Care is not just a school program, Fagan said; it involves many participants and contributors. "Everybody has a role to play, . . . and individuals in the community are there to support those efforts," she said.

Once the coalition has passed through the getting-organized phase, Fagan explained, it enters the third phase, which involves collecting information about the specific issues that need to be addressed in a community. This is done primarily through a school-based survey called the Communities That Care Youth Survey, which is designed to be done in middle and high schools. Youth self-report their exposure to risk factors and protective factors in their communities, families, and schools and among their peers. The results of the surveys can vary substantially from community to community, Fagan said, reflecting different levels of risk and protective factors.

Once the data are collected, she continued, the coalition uses them to create a community action plan aimed at reducing the specific risk factors that are elevated in their communities and at increasing the protective factors that are depressed. Coalition members have a menu of effective evidence-based prevention programs, drawn from the Blueprints for

Healthy Development website, that have already been tested and shown to meet evaluation criteria and to significantly improve youth health and behavior (see Chapter 7). Because the number and range of programs selected are based on community needs, they can differ from community to community, Fagan said.

Schools are often the hardest organizations to convince to adopt new programs, Fagan said, for the reasons cited by Rohrbach and other presenters. But over the 4 years that communities were funded to implement programs, all of them did adopt school programs, she said. Schools were part of the coalitions, and they were partners in efforts to determine what the communities could do, she said.

Communities That Care also helps communities adopt a fidelity-monitoring system that includes training for all program implementers, fidelity "checklists" used by implementers to rate their adherence to the program guidelines, observations to rate the adherence and quality of delivery, documentation of attendance, local monitoring and quality assistance by community coalitions, and external monitoring, Fagan said. "The broad-based implementation monitoring system was not easy to implement," she said. "There was a lot of paperwork, a lot of moving parts, a lot of resistance on the ground. But the upshot was that we had high rates of implementation fidelity across the board" (Fagan et al., 2009).

As an example of how Communities That Care can be scaled up, Fagan briefly described an experience in Pennsylvania where the system was adopted as a statewide initiative beginning in 1994. More than 120 communities have been trained in the system, and there are about 60 coalitions currently active, Fagan said. Nearly 200 evidence-based programs have been replicated, and technical assistance is being provided to the coalitions to support healthy coalition functioning, to ensure high-quality implementation of evidence-based programs, and to promote the sustainability of the coalitions and programs. Fidelity is enhanced by requiring that the program developer visit the site and provide a stamp of approval, Fagan said, and external monitoring keeps the coalitions on track.

In summarizing the effects of Communities That Care, Fagan said that the approach has helped communities identify what works: increase local support for and use of effective prevention services; create an integrated and coordinated system of services; ensure high-quality implementation via structured protocols, continuous quality improvement, and community "pressure"; sustain prevention efforts over time; and realize community-wide reductions in problem behaviors.

The most recent evaluation of sustained changes in youth behaviors showed that communities using the Communities That Care system have substantially increased the number of youth abstaining from alcohol and avoiding delinquency compared to the control communities, Fagan said

(Hawkins et al., 2014). "Those are good outcomes that we hope to continue to see as we follow the kids who have grown up in these communities over time," she said.

## OVERCOMING BARRIERS TO EFFECTIVE IMPLEMENTATION OF BULLYING SCHOOL PREVENTION PROGRAMS

Dissemination and implementation studies can be divided into four categories, said Hendricks Brown, a professor in the Department of Psychiatry and Behavioral Sciences and the Department of Preventive Medicine in the Northwestern University Feinberg School of Medicine. These four categories of studies are exploration, adoption and preparation, implementation, and sustainment. "It is really about making a program work," Brown said. "How do you do that on the ground?"

From a scientific perspective, an important question surrounding implementation is whether it can produce generalizable knowledge. "Is it something that you can take from that particular study and extend and expand to other projects?" Brown asked. The other pertinent question involves local implementation: Can a given program be done locally?

### Challenges to Program Implementation

Brown discussed three challenges in implementing prevention programs in schools. The first was making prevention an integral part of the school mission so that it is sustainable from the very beginning rather than as a last step.

He began by discussing a model developed by Russell Glasgow and his colleagues (1999). The model is known as RE-AIM in reference to its five dimensions:

**Reach**—What proportion of a population is exposed?
**Effectiveness**—Does a program work on outcomes?
**Adoption**—Do organizations take it up?
**Implementation**—Is a program delivered with fidelity?
**Maintenance**—Is a program sustained over time?

One or all of these dimensions can be the subject of research, but all must come together for successful implementation, Brown said. Trying to achieve all five of these aims simultaneously is one of the reasons why implementation can be so difficult, he said.

As an example of making prevention an integral part of the school mission, Brown cited a partnership model developed by Sheppard Kellam (2012) for use in the mental health field. The partnership includes school districts, community organizations, researchers, and policy makers. In these partnerships, Brown said, the intervention program leader serves as the head of the technical and scientific staff. A community board serves as an overseer and adviser to ensure that community values and service agency guidelines are protected, he added.

Kellam developed several steps that need to be taken in establishing these partnerships, and Brown cited three in particular:

1. Analyze which agencies' and community organizations' support is required.
2. Determine the order of engaging with each leader.
3. When trust has been established with each leader, suggest bringing together the needed partners around their determined mutual self-interests in a mutually agreed on site.

An important aspect of this approach, Brown said, is that it does not begin with a research program in search of a school willing to do an intervention. Rather, it takes the form of a collaboration between a school and researchers, with the goal of learning how a prevention program fits into a school's context.

The second challenge that Brown discussed was how best to deliver programs that address multiple prevention targets. To illustrate, he discussed the Good Behavior Game and Familias Unidas. Both of these programs seek to affect drug use, HIV risk behaviors, depressive symptoms, and suicide attempts, he said, and both have produced immediate and long-term positive outcomes, including a reduction in aggression.

The third challenge Brown discussed was building and maintaining a fidelity monitoring system. Schools are normative organizations—that is, they are set up for everybody to attend and are usually not set up to do the detailed work of fidelity assessments, he said. Furthermore, schools generally do not have the resources to develop or maintain fidelity monitoring or feedback systems. However, he said, interventions need both high fidelity and participation by the target audience. Monitoring of fidelity, in turn, has to produce information that is delivered to those delivering the intervention, he said.

To explore this issue, Brown looked again at Familias Unidas, which is a parent-training intervention for middle-school Hispanic youth that is delivered in parent groups in schools and in family visits at home. Currently, school counselors are performing an effectiveness study, with a research team providing monitoring and feedback. But full-scale implementation will require an assessment system for costs, effectiveness, reliability, and fidelity. Given the resource limitations in the school, a decision was made to focus on the issue of joining. This engagement is a key part of the intervention and is common to all interventions. Using computational linguistics with videotapes of sessions, ratings are produced for the training and supervision of counselors. In this way, Brown explained, counselors can learn about, for example, the importance of asking open-ended question. This is just a "a proof of concept," he said. "It is not the whole thing, but it is one of the kinds of ideas that we think ultimately can help."

Brown concluded with several lessons that follow from his research. Prevention needs to further a school's primary mission, he said, with trust and mutual self-interest being established before the research agenda. In addition, he said, programs that have outcomes across multiple dimensions can be prioritized, and monitoring and feedback of a complex behavioral intervention is essential to ensure fidelity.

## FIDELITY VERSUS ADAPTATION

During the discussion session, the conversation continued to center on the issue of whether programs need to be implemented with strict fidelity or can instead be adapted to local circumstances.

One aspect of Communities That Care that promotes fidelity is the amount of planning that goes on before programs are implemented, Fagan said. In choosing programs, one consideration is whether a program can be implemented with fidelity. That way, she said, programs are fitted for a setting so that it is not discovered after implementation that a program is a bad fit for local circumstances. "Communities do not always take the time upfront to think about what they are getting into, and then you are stuck trying to reactively fix the problem and cut corners," she said. "This is one way of trying to avoid the problem."

Rohrbach pointed to an approach in which, after a program is implemented, information is gathered from the implementers about adaptation and ideas for improvement of the program. These data then can be rated according to how consistent they are with a theory of the program. Conclusions that are consistent with the theory can be provided as options for people interested in adapting an intervention, she said. "There are probably a lot of smaller things that we could do in programs to make them more flexible in a planned and strategic way," Rohrbach said. Furthermore, she added, researchers would be interested in such an approach, given their interests in seeing their programs implemented, and such an approach could help researchers identify the aspects of their programs that are most important.

# 11

# Reflections of School Personnel and Student Perspectives

> **Key Points Made by the Individual Speakers**
> - Additional attention to the definition of bullying and policies related to the reporting of bullying could improve preventive efforts. (Cafasso, Dockrey, Dolan, Donlin, Myers)
> - Improving school climate and social norms can be powerful ways to prevent bullying. (Cantave, Farkas, Myers, Shaw)
> - Parents, teachers, and legislators were stakeholders who were missing from the workshop presentations and discussions. (Dockrey, Donlin)
> - Other issues that deserve attention include sibling aggression, self-esteem and self-worth, and recognizing teachers and adults as perpetrators of bullying. (Cafasso, Cantave, Dockrey, Farkas)

One of the final sessions of the workshop included a panel of three school personnel and a second panel of five students who offered their reflections on the workshop presentations and discussions, as well as their thoughts on possible future work on bullying prevention. The panelists were selected to provide a range of viewpoints.

Among the school personnel, the panelists included a high school principal, a coordinator of behavioral supports and interventions for a large public school system, and a program supervisor for a state superintendent's office:

- Virginia Dolan, the coordinator of behavioral supports and interventions for Anne Arundel County Public Schools in Maryland, which is a large system of approximately 120 schools and 80,000 students;
- Mike Donlin, the program supervisor for the School Safety Center of the Office of the Washington State Superintendent of Public Instruction, who works with superintendents, administrators, teachers, parents, and students from 295 school districts and roughly 2,300 individual schools in the state; and
- William Myers, the principal at South River High School, which is the largest high school in Anne Arundel County, Maryland, with about 2,250 students.

Among the student panelists, speakers included current high school students and recent high school graduates from both public and private schools in rural and urban settings:

- Alexa Cafasso, a high school senior at Sacred Heart Academy in Hamden, Connecticut, who instituted a Cyber-Ally Program at her private, all-girls high school to teach leaders how to transition from silent bystanders to local allies;
- Glenn Cantave, a junior at Wesleyan University in Middletown, Connecticut, who was trained as a peer leader in high school to help facilitate anti-bullying activities in local middle schools;
- Whitney Dockrey, a junior at Georgetown University in Washington, DC, who became passionate about bullying prevention when it started to affect people in her school and in her community and was not being addressed;
- Asher Farkas, a sophomore at New York University's Tisch School of the Arts, who was bullied in middle school and transferred to a high school where the environment was more accepting; and
- Rebecca Shaw, a senior at the Horace Mann High School in New York City, who founded an organization called the Anti-Bullying Leadership Network to connect students who care about bullying prevention to researchers who study the issue.

Both panels brought a breadth of experiences and a range of perspectives on bullying prevention that complemented the presentations of research and enriched the overall workshop discussion. Following is a summary of their remarks.

## Definitions

Several of the panelists, including school personnel and students, commented on the need for continued attention to the definition of bullying. Despite the existence of the recently developed uniform definition of bullying (see Chapter 2), definitions and the interpretation of definitions still vary from state to state and jurisdiction to jurisdiction. Furthermore, as Cornell noted, the definitions of bullying used in evidence-based programs may not line up with the definitions of bullying used by schools. Schools would be eager to consider "a clearly publicized, central definition of bullying," said Myers. A common definition could create a starting line for jurisdictions across the country. It also would support accountability, he said, because "what gets checked gets done."

Cafasso pointed out that she goes to a private school, which may interpret and handle bullying in a very different manner than would a public school. A universal definition would make it easier to educate younger children about what bullying is and how to stop it. In addition, a definition that distinguishes cyberbullying from online harassment would be useful, she said.

Dockrey added that youth need information about bullying so they can recognize it for what it is. She explained that bullying may be easy to recognize when a jock is doing it to a nerd, but it can be harder to identify when two girls of the same social class are bullying each other. "That is called 'drama,' but in reality that can become bullying too," she said.

Dolan pointed to a disconnect between parents' understanding and definition of bullying and what school personnel understand to be bullying. Students tend to say that bullying is much more common than is usually reported, she said, which is partly a matter of definitions.

Finally, Donlin talked about the distinctions among harassment, intimidation, and bullying. The three are similar but not the same, he said. They have different impacts and raise different legal implications. To meet state and federal requirements, schools are forced to decide whether a given incident was bullying, harassment, sexual harassment, racial harassment, or something else. Clear understandings are needed to distinguish among different kinds of aggressive acts, he observed.

## Reporting of Bullying

Issues related to reporting bullying were raised by the school personnel panelists. For example, Washington state, which has 295 school districts and about 2,300 individual school buildings, requires a mandated policy on bullying prevention and procedures on prevention and intervention. But how that policy is implemented may vary from school to school, said

Donlin. Every school district writes its own policies and procedures, with guidance provided by the school board association. One exception to this is a state requirement to adopt the state model policy and procedures on harassment, intimidation, and bullying. Although information is annually gathered on programs and trainings provided, there is no process for collecting detailed information on bullying events, anti-bullying program implementation, or investigations of reports of bullying, he said. Although Washington state has a definition, a code of conduct, and a set of responses, an act of bullying can be interpreted as an aggressive fight or disrespect.

Dolan also raised a question about the accuracy of the statistics on bullying. Are elements of bullying masked by other aggressive behaviors? When a school or district has an increased number of bullying incidents, communities can become roused. How can bullying be made a priority for everyone, she asked. In her school system, "soft offenses" such as defiance and disrespect can lead to harder offenses such as fights and attacks. Bullying may be subsumed in different parts of this spectrum of aggressive behaviors, she said.

As Dolan noted, Maryland has a policy regarding reporting of incidents of bullying. However, the system has found inconsistencies between reported incidents and those that have resulted in some sort of disciplinary sanction. It also has found disconnects between what youth are reporting and what adults are reporting, how bullying is perceived and identified, and what is done about it.

Reporting of bullying incidents can create sanctions against schools, noted Dolan, which creates an incentive not to report occurrences. Schools that implement reporting requirements most aggressively can end up with a black eye. In addition, Myers raised the issue of inhibitions for the sharing of information because of legal guidelines. However, he added that his school is very transparent. "We share the data that we collect. It is not a mystery what is happening in our building. That is a model that should flow throughout the county. As we are made more aware of where the challenges are, we can address them," he said.

## School Climate

Several of the student and school personnel panelists focused their remarks on the importance of school climate on bullying prevention. From the student perspective, Farkas said that policies directed toward bullying typically try to put out the fire, but what if steps were taken so that the fires did not get started in the first place? If children could be taught to empathize with others before they even begin elementary school, schools would have far more students who have no need to bully. Research on this topic could point the way to effective programs, he said.

In addition, the environment of schools needs to change, Farkas observed. There is no reason why the social structure of a school needs to resemble a pyramid, with just a few students on top. As noted at the beginning of this workshop summary, Farkas went to both kinds of schools, and the high school he went to was not structured like a pyramid. "There were no popular kids. There were no nerds." If empathy were taught in the classroom by teachers and reinforced by other students, schools would be a better place. "Building from the ground up instead of trying to fix the problems from the surface is a much more effective way of going about things," he said.

Cantave said that teachers should be encouraged to consider why someone is being targeted. If teachers become aware of the vulnerabilities that are being exploited, then they may be able to do something to stop bullying. In addition, the observation that having even one friend reduces the chance of being bullied was "really poignant," said Cantave. Integrating that observation into curricula might help targets become less introverted. If the targets of bullying could be humanized, then other people might step up to defend them when they are being bullied. Cantave also noted that many targets of bullying have low self-esteem, which can have long-term impacts on their lives. Studying these effects could motivate change.

Shaw emphasized the importance of evaluating a school's climate and changing social norms. Empowering a bystander to stand up against bullying can make a big difference, even though it requires social capital. However, the entire system cannot depend on an awkward sixth grader standing up to the cool kid in school. It "is amazing when it happens," she said, "but we cannot build a society on that."

If the norm is to be supportive and not to engage in bullying behavior, then bullying will decrease, said Shaw. In that respect, the examples set by teachers and students leaders are critical. "We must be thinking about the kind of society we are creating." This role modeling cannot come just from teachers and administrators. It needs to be a grassroots movement that resonates with students to become part of the students' norms, she said.

The effect of a heterogeneous social population was interesting, said Shaw, in that it provided a target of bullying with a way of processing an aggressor's actions. More broadly, adjusting the cognitive framework of students might enable many more students to realize why they are being bullied and not blame themselves. "If we can give all students the tools to process it in that way, we can, hopefully, reduce the risks of depression down the line and even cutting down on suicides."

Shaw also pointed to the transition point in late middle school and high school where many anti-bullying programs cease to be effective and can actually be counterproductive. "That makes a lot of sense to me, and it is something that is quite worrisome. It really speaks to changing normative behavior." Teenagers resist being told what to think, she noted. Unless activities like poster campaigns and assemblies are paired with efforts to change the climate, "it ends up coming across as more disingenuous." Given the tools and the facts, students can draw their own conclusions, especially when they are led by adults who know and care about an issue, said Shaw.

From the school perspective, Myers emphasized that bullying cannot and should not be siloed. "It cannot be taken out of context of the total school culture." Creating social norms for peer groups within the schoolhouse is extremely important, he said. Donlin agreed. He said that the school climate is a fundamental consideration. "When I am doing my work in bullying prevention with districts or schools or families or parents, one of the first things I tell people is that bullying is a community event and it takes a community to deal with it." Preventive activities can help create that climate and need to be done upfront, with awareness as the first step in prevention, he said.

### Program Implementation

School personnel often feel what Myers called "implementation anxiety" over getting a program accepted and then implemented with fidelity at the school level. School personnel face many barriers in implementing programs, as pointed out by several presenters, including the number of mandated "must-dos" that have to be taken into consideration. Furthermore, the county does not have a systemic program for all schools to follow, Myers said, so each school individually considers what would work best.

A difficult question that school personnel face is what to do after a bullying incident, Myers observed. What can be done for a bullied child, and what should be done to a child exhibiting bullying behaviors? How can prevention be maintained going forward? Not having such interventions can have long-lasting and costly impacts, he said.

Dolan also noted that schools can implement programs without fidelity and then wonder why they do not work. Planning is required to implement a program successfully, she said. In particular, the climate of a school is a strong determinant of what can and cannot be done. Schools need to be more accountable for the implementation of programs, Dolan continued. One positive aspect of Positive Behavioral Interventions and Supports, a bullying prevention program used in the Anne Arundel school system, is that it does hold schools accountable. Schools are given a score around implementation, and the scores have been tied to incentives for the school, she noted.

Dealing with bullying also requires training, Donlin said, even though no separate, dedicated funding is available in his state to provide training.

In addition, training tends to focus on policies and procedures rather than on prevention or best practices. But educators need help developing the skills to create safe and secure learning environments for all students in all settings, he noted.

Legislators need to hear what works, how programs can be implemented, and how they can be taken to scale, observed Donlin. They also need to know that implementing such programs at scale requires time, funding, people, and other resources.

### The Biological Evidence

The biological evidence was mesmerizing, Myers observed. Research shows that long-term stress can have dramatic effects on the adolescent brain, but recovery is also possible if the right interventions are available, he noted. The biological findings help avoid a tendency to blame the victim, Dolan added.

The students, like the school personnel, were impressed by the potential of the biological evidence on bullying to influence opinions. Cantave pointed out, for example, that the biological observations could keep students from being marginalized, because others might realize that they have undergone traumatic experiences, as reflected by changes in their brain. More research on the long-term damages of bullying could greatly increase the potential impact of these observations, Dockrey added.

### Technology and Other Resources

In a highly technological culture, a variety of technologies can influence the attitudes and knowledge of students. For example, Cafasso noted that public service notices can be a powerful way of influencing school climates. The MTV commercials that point to the thin line between words and wounds are an example of messages that can make "a huge difference," she said.

Students of different ages use different social media and technologies, Dockrey noted, which requires that anti-bullying messages travel through different outlets. Messages also need to be paired with what teens want and need to hear, she noted.

Technologies offer a possible way of encouraging and supporting students to make friends, said Dockrey. "Even if they do not have a friend at their school, they are at least going to be able to know that they have a friend in that organization one county over and they can text and talk and Facebook with that person all they want."

To reduce cyberbullying, some schools encourage their teachers and administrators to be online, Farkas noted. Having a teacher to whom a student can reach out for help can be very valuable during stressful periods, he said.

The http://www.stopbullying.gov website has been a "tremendous resource" to Shaw in her capacity as the president of the Anti-Bullying Leadership Network. She often receives e-mails and Facebook messages from parents or students asking how they can respond to bullying. The website is respectful to students, has pages directed toward students of different ages, provides important facts, and presents the options for different locations, Shaw said.

Until 10 or 15 years ago, bullying did not get much attention, she continued. Its increased visibility means that more ideas and materials are available, and it can be hard to sort through those materials. The push toward data-driven methods and programs that have been rigorously tested helps greatly in that regard, and more evidence-based programs are needed. "It really does seem like we are on the precipice of making a big difference," Shaw said.

Myers agreed with the student panelists that technology is a major influence on the lives of children and adolescents. But schools still do not have technology-enabled programs available to them that could deliver the message of bullying to parents in the community. "That would be invaluable to have," he said. Another valuable resource would be a program beginning at the elementary level to teach students about the appropriate use of technology and about some of the pitfalls that can occur.

Myers also asked whether parents can be provided with concrete guidelines for help with a bullied child. A program or even a pamphlet about what they can do in such a situation would be very helpful, he said.

## Missing Stakeholders

School personnel and student panelists were asked to reflect on stakeholders and issues that they felt were missing from the workshop presentations and discussions. Donlin identified legislators as a stakeholder group not represented at the workshop. In his job, he deals often with legislators, whether at a local level or a state level. "We have a very good state law and good policy," he said, "but the challenge is to make sure that everything is practical and practicable."

Another group missing from the workshop was school personnel involved in special education and 504 plans under the Rehabilitation Act and the Americans with Disabilities Act, he noted. The students who are covered by those programs also need to be protected, Donlin said.

Dockrey said that one group missing from the conversation at the workshop was parents. Parents need to be equipped to respond well when their children come to them with bullying problems, she said. Some parents look for their own identity and status in the accomplishments of their children. They may not want to hear that their children are having problems with bullying, because it implies that they have done something wrong. Parents can build their children's self-esteem by getting them involved in organizations and supporting their activities. Dockrey suggested that parents can help their children establish relationships, especially because parents are the first people with whom children experience love. "If they don't get these skills at home, then they are not going to be able to take them into schools to make that one friend or the relationships that they need," Dockrey said.

## Other Issues

Finally, the student and school personnel panelists were asked to consider issues that were not raised during the workshop presentations and that were missing from the overall discussion. This section summarizes several topics that were raised.

### *Teachers and Adults as Bullies*

Several of the student respondents pointed out that, as Farkas said, "teachers can be bullies, too." The definition of bullying should not limit itself just to youth, Farkas continued. In his high school, students did not bully each other, but teachers did bully students. "We had chemistry teachers calling their kids 'stupid.' We had English teachers calling out racial slurs, sexual orientation slurs. . . . That is straight-up bullying." When Farkas complained to administrators about a particular teacher, the teacher was not disciplined and Farkas was sent to another classroom. "I was glad to no longer be in the classroom. But the way that looked to the rest of the school population is that I was being punished for being bullied."

Teachers have their own biases, and they can act as models for bullying among students. "If teachers are giving the impression that this kind of behavior is okay, the kids are going to think this kind of behavior is okay." Teachers need the same kind of bullying prevention training that students receive, Farkas said.

Dockrey observed that bullying may take the form of a teacher who only acknowledges the jocks and popular students at school. What teachers think about students is going to shape their self-identity, she added. "We cannot be having teachers and coaches being okay with bullying kids in addition to the students who are doing so." The research on changes in the brain can help them recognize the damage they are doing to students. When teachers or administrators label a student a "drama queen," that is just an easy way not to address a problem, Dockrey said. Cafasso also mentioned the importance of adults bullying youth. Research on teachers, coaches, family members, or other adults involved in bullying youth could help explore this largely overlooked behavior, she said.

*Sibling Aggression*

Sibling aggression can be a factor in bullying, Dockrey noted, because how a child feels at home is how he or she is going to act in the wider world. If children are loved and confident at home, then they will feel confident and loved at school. Dockrey has three younger sisters, and if something bad happens to one of them at school, "they are going to come back to three other best friends. I think if we can instill that into families, that could significantly help them as they are going out into schools and having to deal with these issues."

*Self-Esteem and Self-Worth*

Finally, an issue largely overlooked by the workshop, according to Cantave, was the importance of self-esteem and confidence on the part of victims. As adolescents spend more time with computers than with family or friends, sources of reinforcement, such as "likes" on Facebook, can become extremely important in the social life of teens. "But those who are targeted, those who are marginalized, they are not getting those Facebook likes. . . . Where are you getting that validation? Where are you getting that self-worth? That is a really big issue." A self-worth campaign could change the environment, he suggested. "Quirks seen as oddities to some could be passions for others. Somehow, somewhere, we need to eliminate the importance of external validation and have people really recognize their self-worth," Cantave said.

# 12

# Final Thoughts

In the final session of the workshop, the members of the planning committee discussed themes from the workshop sessions and individual presentations as well as promising areas for future research and policy action. Their comments are summarized here not as the conclusions of the workshop but as an overview of the issues discussed.

## BULLYING AND VICTIMIZATION AND THE TARGETS OF BULLYING

Perspectives on bullying and the approaches taken to prevent and respond to it can differ from place to place because of competing priorities, issues related to accountability, and differences in the implementation of policies and programs, as Catherine Bradshaw observed. A uniform definition of bullying has recently been developed, but that definition has not necessarily been incorporated at the local level, she added. Bradshaw also mentioned that bullying prevention is often imposed as an unfunded mandate. "Until we are able to dedicate the funding and set this issue of bullying prevention as a priority, we are not going to get a lot of traction," she said.

Many presentations had emphasized the importance of context, Bradshaw observed, including such contextual factors as cultural differences, dating relationships, urban-versus-rural settings, cyberbullying, and families, to name just a few. Developmental factors are also important, given that the types of effective interventions will vary across the lifecourse, Bradshaw said. Another theme that came up repeatedly over the course of the 2 days was the importance of connectedness, whether that takes the form of a relationship with a peer or an adult who can act as a buffer to bullying. Researchers need a better way of operationalizing and incorporating such contextual factors into their studies, Bradshaw said. "Rarely are we able to walk away with a good statistical model that maps on to what people actually are seeing in real life."

Bradshaw also brought up the issue of diversity, whether ethnic, cultural, physical, or sexual. As noted in Chapter 1, this issue was intended to be integrated in presentations throughout the workshop rather than being addressed in a single session, because it is a major consideration in bullying prevention.

Several planning committee members commented on the neurobiological underpinnings of responses to bullying that researchers are starting to uncover, as presented by Vaillancourt (see Chapter 2). These biological studies help to explain the idea of allostatic load, Bradshaw said, in which prior experiences with stress and trauma make it more challenging for someone to rebound from additional stress. Megan Moreno also pointed to the power of the demonstrated biological changes to motivate an intervention platform with parents and teachers.

## SCHOOL-BASED INTERVENTIONS

There is still no solid base of evidence for many of the bullying prevention interventions being implemented in schools, Denise Gottfredson pointed out. Randomized controlled trials are difficult to conduct in schools, but some results from school-based studies have been very positive. School policies sometimes diminish the significance of bullying, she added, which makes bullying issues harder to address. Also, high-profile media events tend to dominate the public's and administrators' attention, which can result in resources being diverted into school security measures and zero-tolerance policies, even though homicides in schools are actually very rare, she noted.

Gottfredson and several other planning committee members called attention to the importance of school climate in bullying prevention. For example, the student-to-teacher ratio can have an effect on bullying, as can the role of other stakeholders in the school setting and the norms held by students and adults for that school. Presentations by Dodge and Faris highlighted that how schools are engineered and organized can have an influence on peer interactions and aggressive peer behaviors. Anti-bullying campaigns, role modeling, peer relationships, and positive approaches all can make a big difference by shaping school climates, Gottfredson said. Presentations by Bradshaw and Juvonen pointed to examples from the research of how to develop a climate of inclusion and support. In addition,

Moreno called attention to the fact that the young people who spoke at the workshop (see Chapter 11) identified the school climate as a contributing factor to whether bullying takes place. For example, student panelists Farkas and Shaw suggested that school climate can have a major impact on how students experience or intervene in bullying behavior. Finally, several presenters noted that even one friend or supporter, whether a peer or teacher, can make a difference to a victimized young person.

Gottfredson suggested that a working group could identify the most promising components of a multi-component approach to bullying prevention in schools. Important components of such an approach could be involving more people in the school community, especially high-status students, as part of the solution; starting with the adults in schools to clarify norms about bullying; promoting meaningful connections among individuals within schools; and reorganizing the way students are grouped for instruction. Todres also emphasized the need to focus on structural issues, especially contextual factors, and on the importance of incentives for schools.

## FAMILY-FOCUSED INTERVENTIONS

Todres emphasized that parents and other caregivers are essential partners in successful interventions. However, the rates of bullying reported by parents are less than the rates their children report. Parents also think that their children will tell them if they are being bullied, whereas children report that they are less likely to report bullying than their parents believe. Finally, children report more social and health impacts than parents perceive. "That suggests an area of need both for research and for further interventions," Todres said.

Families can serve as sources of risk, protection factors, or managers of contextual risk, Todres continued. Nurturing parenting skills, fostering stable family relationships, ensuring appropriate supervision of children, encouraging parental involvement in school, and connecting families with neighborhoods and social supports all can increase the ability of parents to deal with bullying, he said.

## TECHNOLOGY-BASED INTERVENTIONS

The vast majority of youth today are online, along with ever growing populations of adults, Moreno said. These online communities can be both a source of interventions and preventive measures and a place where bullying can occur. Many youth access health information online, especially information about topics that they might find stigmatizing or embarrassing to ask about in public. "This may be a place where youth who have been bullied would feel more comfortable seeking help or support," Moreno said.

As in other areas of bullying prevention, little evidence exists demonstrating the efficacy of online bullying intervention. But the knowledge base about school-based interventions in general could guide thinking about how to structure and test an online intervention. Young people themselves can partner with adults in understanding what might and might not work, Moreno suggested.

## COMMUNITY-BASED INTERVENTIONS

Other programs and frameworks, such as the Big Brothers and Big Sisters program and Communities That Care, have demonstrated the potential of community-based programs to improve health, Nina Fredland observed. Pediatricians and other health care professionals can make important contributions to bullying prevention efforts while also identifying and providing assistance to students who are suffering from negative health outcomes related to bullying. For example, the American Academy of Pediatrics has identified injury prevention, including bullying prevention, as a public health issue. The role of primary health care providers in this area could be even greater if it were possible to share information between providers and key school personnel such as school nurses, social workers, and school psychologists, within the context of confidentiality, Fredland said.

Moreno emphasized the importance of community and stakeholder buy-in. "These are people we should be bringing to the table at every stage of our research projects and not waiting until the implementation stage," she said. "We could get so much more information about what might work and what theoretical models are resonating with the people who are going to be implementing these and affected by these."

## PEER-LED AND PEER-FOCUSED PROGRAMS

Bullying is a proactive rather than reactive form of aggression, Todres observed, and youth often use it to try to achieve higher status within social groups. This is one reason why it can be counterproductive for interventions to place youth who bully with each other in groups, because these groups can exacerbate rather than reduce bullying. Instead, interventions that support adult involvement, positive relationships, self-regulation, and group management skills are most likely to have positive effects on problem behaviors, Todres said. Preventing the formation of gangs, early intervention, and a peer culture of nonaggression also can prevent bullying, he observed.

## LAWS AND PUBLIC POLICIES

Most state legislatures have passed anti-bullying laws over the past 15 years, Todres pointed out. However, these laws vary greatly from state to state and also within states, because many of the laws delegate authority to school boards and schools to establish policies.

Inclusive anti-bullying policies are associated with a reduced risk of peer victimization for all youth, and laws and policies can support training programs, improvements in school culture, and other positive interventions. However, laws and policies also can hinder enforcement, because schools fear that they will be sued by the parents of students accused of bullying, and legislation can run afoul of privacy laws. As in many areas of bullying prevention, more research is needed both on the effectiveness of laws and policies and on their successful implementation, Todres said.

## TRANSLATING BULLYING RESEARCH INTO POLICY AND PRACTICE

"All of our good work to develop effective bullying prevention interventions will be for naught if we cannot ensure that they are implemented with reasonable fidelity on the ground and are sustained over a long period of time," Gottfredson said. Particular characteristics of programs or policies can increase the likelihood that they could be implemented with high fidelity; these characteristics include clear messages, solid technical training, and technical assistance. More challenging but equally important is building a local infrastructure in the community to select evidence-based practices and deliver them with fidelity. Key aspects of this infrastructure are strong leadership, administrative support, and the presence of a program champion at the local level, Gottfredson said. Such an infrastructure also can increase the capacity to monitor implementation and feed that information back to local implementers.

Interventions that address risk factors for a variety of different problem behaviors often receive more local support than more narrowly focused programs, Gottfredson observed. For example, programs to improve school climate by increasing the clarity of norms at the school level and enhancing discipline management can be beneficial across the board and not just for bullying, she said.

The field of bullying prevention can learn from other fields of research and practice, Todres said, and some of the research that was reviewed and discussed drew on work from related topics (e.g., violence and aggression). However, Limber and other presenters were careful to note that while bullying overlaps with these other constructs, it is also distinct in important respects. Consequently, the extent to which this research on related topics applies to bullying is an open question. Another gap in the research, Gottfredson added, is how to scale up programs effectively and produce benefits in real-world settings. Bradshaw added that researchers need to devote increased attention to the mediators and moderators of bullying and anti-bullying interventions. Partnerships between researchers who are fielding randomized trials and methodologists can yield better and more information about what works under different conditions, she noted.

As Frederick Rivara, chair of the planning committee for the workshop, said during his introductory remarks, he bases his actions and beliefs on the premise that all injuries are preventable. Bullying is not just something that children and adolescents always have done and always will do. Bullying and the consequences of bullying to the victim, the perpetrators, schools, and society can be prevented. "It is up to us to act," he said.

# Appendixes

# A

# References

AAP (American Academy of Pediatrics). 2014. Connected kids: Safe, strong, secure. http://www2.aap.org/connectedkids (accessed May 21, 2014).

Abrams, D. E. 2009. A coordinated public response to school bullying. In M. R. Dyson and D. B. Weddle (Eds.), *Our promise: Achieving educational equity for America's children* (pp. 399–423). Durham, NC: Carolina Academic Press.

Abrams, D. E. 2012. Bullying as a disability in public elementary and secondary education. *Missouri Law Review* 77:781–804.

Abrams, D. E. 2013. School bullying victimization as an educational disability. *Temple Political & Civil Rights Law Review* 22:273–290.

APA (American Psychological Association) Zero Tolerance Task Force. 2008. Are zero tolerance policies effective in the schools?: An evidentiary review and recommendations. *American Psychologist* 63:852–862.

Basile, K. C., D. L. Espelage, I. Rivers, P. M. McMahon, and T. R. Simon. 2009. The theoretical and empirical links between bullying behavior and sexual violence perpetration. *Aggression and Violent Behavior* 14(5):336–347.

Bellmore, A. D., M. Witkow, S. Graham, and J. Juvonen. 2004. Beyond the individual: The impact of ethnic context and classroom behavioral norms on victims' adjustment. *Developmental Psychology* 40:1159–1172.

Benjet, C., R. J. Thompson, and I. H. Gotlib. 2010. 5-HTTLPR moderates the effect of relational peer victimization on depressive symptoms in adolescent girls. *Journal of Child Psychology and Psychiatry* 51(2):173–179.

Borum, R., D. Cornell, W. Modzeleski, and S. R. Jimerson. 2010. What can be done about school shootings? A review of the evidence. *Educational Researcher* 39:27–37.

Bradshaw, C. P., W. M. Reinke, L. D. Brown, K. B. Bevans, and P. J. Leaf. 2008. Implementation of school-wide positive behavioral interventions and supports (PBIS) in elementary schools: Observations from a randomized trial. *Education and Treatment of Children* 31(1):1–26.

Buhs, E. S., G. W. Ladd, and S. L. Herald. 2006. Peer exclusion and victimization: Processes that mediate the relation between peer group rejection and children's classroom engagement and achievement? *Journal of Educational Psychology* 98:1–13.

Buhs, E. S., G. W. Ladd, and S. L. Herald-Brown. 2010. Victimization and exclusion: Links to peer rejection, classroom engagement, and achievement. In S. R. Jimerson, S. M. Swearer, and D. L. Espelage (Eds.), *The handbook of school bullying: An international perspective* (pp. 163–172). New York: Routledge.

Caspi, A., K. Sugden, T. E. Moffitt, A. Taylor, I. W. Craig, H. Harrington, J. McClay, J. Mill, J. Martin, A. Braithwaite, and R. Poulton. 2003. Influence of life stress on depression: Moderation by a polymorphism in the 5-HTT gene. *Science* 301(5631):386–389.

CDC (Centers for Disease Control and Prevention). 2012. Suicide: Facts at a glance. http://www.cdc.gov/ViolencePrevention/pdf/Suicide_DataSheet-a.pdf (accessed May 21, 2014).

CDC. 2014a. National Center for Health Statistics. http://www.cdc.gov/nchs (accessed May 21, 2014).

CDC. 2014b. School Associated Violent Death Surveillance Study. http://www.cdc.gov/violence prevention/youthviolence/schoolviolence/savd.html (accessed May 21, 2014).

Chen, Z., K. D. Williams, J. Fitness, and N. C. Newton. 2008. When hurt will not heal: Exploring the capacity to relive social and physical pain. *Psychological Science* 19(8):789–795.

Cohen, J. 2009. Transforming school climate: Educational and psychoanalytic perspectives. *Schools: Studies in Education* 6:99–103.

Cohen, J., L. McCabe, N. M. Michelli, and T. Pickeral. 2009. School climate: Research, policy, practice, and teacher education. *Teachers College Record* 111:180–213.

Cohen, M. A., and A. R. Piquero. 2009. New evidence on the monetary value of saving a high risk youth. *Journal of Quantitative Criminology* 25:25–49.

Cohen, M. A., A. R. Piquero, and W. G. Jennings. 2010. Estimating the costs of bad outcomes for at-risk youth and the benefits of early childhood interventions to reduce them. *Criminal Justice Policy Review* 21(4):391–434.

Cook, C. R., K. R. Williams, N. G. Guerra, and T. E. Kim. 2010a. Variability in the prevalence of bullying and victimization: A cross-national and methodological analysis. In S. R. Jimerson, S. M. Swearer, and D. L. Espelage (Eds.), *Handbook of bullying in schools: An international perspective* (pp. 347–362). New York: Routledge.

Cook, P. J., D. C. Gottfredson, and C. Na. 2010b. School crime control and prevention. *Crime and Justice* 39(1):313–440.

Copeland, W. E., D. Wolke, A. Angold, and E. J. Costello. 2013. Adult psychiatric outcomes of bullying and being bullied by peers in childhood and adolescence. *JAMA Psychiatry* 70:419–426.

Cornell, D. 2006. *School violence: Fears versus facts*. Mahwah, NJ: Lawrence Erlbaum.

Cornell, D., and J. Cole. 2011. Assessment of bullying. In S.R. Jimerson, A. B. Nickerson, M. J. Mayer, and M. J. Furlong (Eds.), *The handbook of school violence and school safety: International research and practice, 2nd edition* (pp. 289–303). Mahwah, NJ: Routledge.

Crowley, M. J., J. Wu, C. A. Bailey, and L. C. Mayes. 2009. Bringing in the negative reinforcements: The avoidance feedback-related negativity. *Neuroreport* 20(17):1513–1517.

Dahlberg, L., and E. Krug. 2002. Violence: A global health problem. In E. Krug, L. Dahlberg, J. Mercy, A. Zwi, and R. Lozano (Eds.), *World report on violence and health* (pp. 3–21). Geneva: World Health Organization.

DeAngelis, K. J., B. O. Brent, and D. Ianni. 2011. The hidden cost of school security. *Journal of Education Finance* 36:312–337.

Dijkstra, J. K., S. Lindenberg, R. Veenstra, C. Steglich, J. Isaacs, N. A. Card, and E. V. Hodges. 2010. Influence and selection processes in weapon carrying during adolescence: The roles of status, aggression, and vulnerability. *Criminology* 48(1):187–220.

Dishion, T. J., S. E. Nelson, and M. Yasui. 2005. Predicting early adolescent gang involvement from middle school adaptation. *Journal of Clinical Child and Adolescent Psychology* 34:62–73.

Dodge, K. A., and M. R. Sherrill. 2006. Deviant peer-group effects in youth mental health interventions. In K. A. Dodge, T. J. Dishion, and J. E. Lansford (Eds.), *Deviant peer influences in programs for youth: Problems and solutions* (pp. 97–121). New York: Guilford.

DoSomething.org. 2014. Bully text. https://www.dosomething.org/bullytext (accessed May 23, 2014).

Durlak, J. A., and E. P. Dupre. 2008. Implementation matters: A review of research on the influence of implementation on program outcomes and the factors affecting the implementation. *American Journal of Community Psychology* 41:327–350.

Eaton, D. K., L. Kann, S. Kinchen, S. Shanklin, J. Ross, J. Hawkins, W. A. Harris, R. Lowry, T. McManus, D. Chyen, C. Lim, L. Whittle, N. D. Brener, and H. Wechsler. 2009. Youth risk behavior surveillance—United States, 2009. *Morbidity and Mortality Weekly Report Surveillance Summaries* 59(5):1–142.

Eaton, D. K., L. Kann, S. Kinchen, S. Shanklin, K. H. Flint, J. Hawkins, W. A. Harris, R. Lowry, T. McManus, D. Chyen, L. Whittle, C. Lim, and H. Wechsler. 2012. Youth risk behavior surveillance—United States, 2011. *Morbidity and Mortality Weekly Report Surveillance Summaries* 61(4):1–162. http://www.cdc.gov/mmwr/preview/mmwrhtml/ss6104a1.htm (accessed May 19, 2014).

Eliot, M., D. Cornell, A. Gregory, and X. Fan. 2010. Supportive school climate and student willingness to seek help for bullying and threats of violence. *Journal of School Psychology* 48(6):533–553.

Espelage, D. L., and S. M. Swearer. 2010. A social-ecological model for bullying prevention and intervention: Understanding the impact of adults in the social ecology of youngsters. In S. R. Jimerson, S. M. Swearer, and D. L. Espelage (Eds.), *Handbook of bullying in schools: An international perspective* (pp. 61–72). New York: Routledge.

Espelage, D. L., K. Bosworth, and T. R. Simon. 2000. Examining the social context of bullying behaviors in early adolescence. *Journal of Counseling & Development* 78:326–333.

Espelage, D. L., K. C. Basile, and M. E. Hamburger. 2012. Bullying perpetration and subsequent sexual violence perpetration among middle school students. *Journal of Adolescent Health* 50:60–65.

Espelage, D. L., S. Low, M. A. Rao, J. S. Hong, and T. Little. 2013. Family violence, bullying, fighting, and substance use among adolescents: A longitudinal transactional model. *Journal of Research on Adolescence* 24(2):337–349. doi: 10.1111/jora.12060.

Espelage, D. L., S. K. Low, C. Anderson, and L. De La Rue. 2014. Bullying, sexual, and dating violence trajectories from early to late adolescence. Report submitted to the National Institute of Justice Grant #2011-MU-FX-0022.

Espelage, D. L., K. C. Basile, M. E. Hamburger, and L. De La Rue. In press. Longitudinal associations among bully, homophobic teasing and sexual violence perpetration among middle school students. *Journal of Interpersonal Violence*.

Espinoza, G. Under Review. Daily Cyberbullying Experiences: Links with Emotional, Physical and School Adjustment.

Fagan, A. A., K. Hanson, J. D. Hawkins, and M. Arthur. 2009. Translational research in action: Implementation of the Communities That Care Prevention System in 12 communities. *Journal of Community Psychology* 37(7):809–829.

Faris, R. 2012. Aggression, exclusivity, and status attainment in interpersonal networks. *Social Forces* 90:1207–1235.

Faris, R., and S. Ennett. 2012. Adolescent aggression: The role of peer group status motives, peer aggression, and group characteristics. *Social Networks* 34(4):371–378.

Faris, R., and D. Felmlee. 2011. Status struggles network centrality and gender segregation in same- and cross-gender aggression. *American Sociological Review* 76(1):48–73.

Faris, R., and D. Felmlee. 2014. Casualties of social combat: School networks of peer victimization and their consequences. *American Sociological Review* 79(2):228–257. doi: 10.1177/0003122414524573.

Farmer, T. W., J. V. Hamm, K. L. Lane, D. Lee, K. S. Sutherland, C. M. Hall, and R. A. Murray. 2013. Conceptual foundations and components of a contextual intervention to promote student engagement during early adolescence: The Supporting Early Adolescent Learning and Social Success (SEALS) model. *Journal of Educational and Psychological Consultation* 23:115–139.

Farrington, D., and M. Ttofi. 2009. School based programs to reduce bullying and victimization: A systematic review. *Campbell Systematic Reviews* 5(6).

Fekkes, M., F. I. Pijpers, and S. P. Verloove-Vanhorick. 2005. Bullying: Who does what, when and where? Involvement of children, teachers and parents in bullying behavior. *Health Education Research* 20(1):81–91.

Finkelhor, D., H. Turner, R. Ormrod, and S. L. Hamby. 2009. Violence, abuse, and crime exposure in a national sample of children and youth. *Pediatrics* 124:1411–1423.

Foshee, V. A., K. E. Bauman, S. T. Ennett, C. Suchindran, T. Benefield, and G. F. Linder. 2005. Assessing the effects of dating violence prevention program "Safe Dates" using random coefficient regression modeling. *Prevention Science* 6(3):245–257.

Gini, G., and T. Pozzoli. 2013. Bullied children and psychosomatic problems: A meta-analysis. *Pediatrics* 132:720–729.

Gladden, R. M., A. M. Vivolo-Kantor, M. E. Hamburger, and C. D. Lumpkin. 2014. *Bullying surveillance among youth: Uniform definitions for public health and recommended data elements, version 1.0*. Atlanta, GA: National Center for Injury Prevention and Control, Centers for Disease Control and Prevention and U.S. Department of Education. http://www.cdc.gov/violenceprevention/pdf/bullying-definitions-final-a.pdf (accessed May 19, 2014).

Glasgow, R. E., T. M. Vogt, and S. M. Boles. 1999. Evaluating the public health impact of health promotion interventions: The RE-AIM Framework. *American Journal of Public Health* 89:1322–1327.

Glasgow, R. E., E. Lichtenstein, and A. C. Marcus. 2003. Why don't we see more translation of health promotion research to practice? Rethinking the efficacy–effectiveness transition. *American Journal of Public Health* 93(8):1261–1267.

Gottfredson, D. C. 1986. An empirical test of school-based environmental and individual interventions to reduce the risk of delinquent behavior. *Criminology* 24:705–731.

Gottfredson, D. C. 1990. Changing school structures to benefit high risk youths. In P. E. Leone (Ed.), *Understanding troubled and troubling youth: Multidisciplinary perspectives*. Newbury Park, CA: Sage.

Gottfredson, D. C., and S. M. DiPietro. 2011. School size, social capital, and student victimization. *Sociology of Education* 84:69–89.

Gottfredson, G. D., and D. C. Gottfredson. 1985. *Victimization in schools*. New York: Plenum.

Gottfredson, G. D., D. C. Gottfredson, A. A. Payne, and N. C. Gottfredson. 2005. School climate predictors of school disorder: Results from the national study of delinquency prevention in schools. *Journal of Research in Crime and Delinquency* 42(4):412–444.

Graham, S., A. Bellmore, A. Nishina, and J. Juvonen. 2009. "It must be me": Ethnic context and attributions for peer victimization. *Journal of Youth and Adolescence* 38:487–499.

Gregory, A., D. Cornell, X. Fan, P. Sheras, and T. Shih. 2010. Authoritative school discipline: High school practices associated with lower student bullying and victimization. *Journal of Educational Psychology* 102:483–496.

Gross, E. F. 2009. Logging on, bouncing back: An experimental investigation of online communication following social exclusion. *Developmental Psychology* 45:1787–1793.

Hatzenbuehler, M. L., and K. M. Keyes. 2013. Inclusive anti-bullying policies and reduced risk of suicide attempts in lesbian and gay youth. *Journal of Adolescent Health* 53(1 Suppl):21–26.

Hatzenbuehler, M. L., K. M. Keyes, and D. S. Hasin. 2009. State-level policies and psychiatric morbidity in lesbian, gay, and bisexual populations. *American Journal of Public Health* 99(12):2275–2281.

Hatzenbuehler, M. L., K. A. McLaughlin, K. M. Keyes, and D. S. Hasin. 2010. The impact of institutional discrimination on psychiatric disorders in lesbian, gay, and bisexual populations: A prospective study. *American Journal of Public Health* 100(3):452–459.

Hatzenbuehler, M. L., C. O'Cleirigh, C. Grasso, K. Mayer, S. Safren, and J. Bradford. 2012. Effect of same-sex marriage laws on health care use and expenditures in sexual minority men: A quasi-natural experiment. *American Journal of Public Health* 102(2):285–291.

Hawkins, J. D., S. Oesterle, E. C. Brown, K. C. Monahan, R. D. Abbott, M. W. Arthur, and R. F. Catalano. 2012. Sustained decreases in risk exposure and youth problem behaviors after installation of the Communities That Care prevention system in a randomized trial. *Archives of Pediatrics and Adolescent Medicine* 166(2):141–148.

Hawkins, J. D., S. Oesterle, E. C. Brown, R. D. Abbott, and R. F. Catalano. 2014. Youth problem behaviors 8 years after implementing the communities that care prevention system: A community-randomized trial. *JAMA Pediatrics* 168(2):122–129.

HBSC (Health Behavior in School-Aged Children). 2013. *2009–2010 Student survey. Analysis ran on 2014-03-11 using SDA 3.5: Tables.* http://www.icpsr.umich.edu/icpsrweb/ICPSR/studies/34792 (accessed March 11, 2014).

Henry, D. 2013. Multisite Violence Prevention Project. The moderating role of developmental microsystems in selective preventive intervention effects on aggression and victimization of aggressive and socially influential students. *Prevention Science* 14(4):390–399.

Hertz, M., I. Donato, and J. Wright. 2013. Bullying and suicide: A public health approach. *Journal of Adolescent Health* 53(1):S1–S3.

Hogeveen, J., M. Inzlicht,, and S. S. Obhi. 2014. Power changes how the brain responds to others. *Journal of Experimental Psychology: General* 143(2):755.

Holt, M. K., G. Kaufman Kantor, and D. Finkelhor. 2008. Parent/child concordance about bullying involvement and family characteristics related to bullying and peer victimization. *Journal of School Violence* 8(1):42–63. doi: 10.1080/15388220802067813. http://dx.doi.org/10.1080/15388220802067813 (accessed May 20, 2014).

Houndoumadi, A., and L. Pateraki. 2001. Bullying and bullies in Greek elementary schools: Pupils' attitudes and teachers'/parents' awareness. *Educational Review* 53(1):19–26. doi:10.1080/00131910120033619.

Iannotti, R. J. 2014. *Health behavior in school-aged children (HBSC), 2009–2010.* ICPSR34792-v1. Ann Arbor, MI: Inter-University Consortium for Political and Social Research [distributor], 2013-11-20. doi:10.3886/ICPSR34792.v1. http://www.icpsr.umich.edu/icpsrweb/ICPSR/studies/34792 (accessed May 19, 2014).

IOM (Institute of Medicine) and NRC (National Research Council). 2003. *Deadly lessons: Understanding lethal school violence.* Washington, DC: The National Academies Press.

Juvonen, J., A. Nishina, and S. Graham. 2006. Ethnic diversity and perceptions of safety in urban middle schools. *Psychological Science* 17:393–400.

Karch, D. L., J. Logan, D. D. McDaniel, C. F. Floyd, and K. J. Vagi. 2013. Precipitating circumstances of suicide among youth aged 10–17 years by sex: Data from the National Violent Death Reporting System, 16 states, 2005–2008. *Journal of Adolescent Health* 53:51–53.

Kellam, S. G. 2012. Developing and maintaining partnerships as the foundation of implementation and implementation science: Reflections over a half century. *Administration and Policy in Mental Health and Mental Health Services Research* 39(4):317–320.

Kellam, S. G., A. C. L. Mackenzie, C. H. Brown, J. M. Poduska, W. Wang, H. Petras, and H. C. Wilcox. 2011. The good behavior game and the future of prevention and treatment. *Addiction Science and Clinical Practice* 6:73–84.

Kerner, J. F., and K. L. Hall. 2009. Research dissemination and diffusion: Translation within science and society. *Research on Social Work Practice* 19(5):519–530.

Kerr, D. C. R., L. D. Leve, and P. Chamberlain. 2009. Pregnancy rates among juvenile justice girls in two RCTs of multidimensional treatment foster care. *Journal of Consulting and Clinical Psychology* 77(3):588–593. doi: 10.1037/a0015289.

Klomek, A. B., M. Kleinman, E. Altschuler, F. Marrocco, L. Amakawa, and M. S. Gould. 2013. Suicidal adolescents' experiences with bullying perpetration and victimization during high school as risk factors for later depression and suicidality. *Journal of Adolescent Health* 53(1 Suppl):S37–S42.

Leff, S. S., D. E. Thomas, N. A. Vaughn, N. A. Thomas, J. Paquette MacEvoy, M. A. Freedman, S. Abdul-Kabir, J. Woodlock, T. Guerra, A. S. Bradshaw, E. M. Woodburn, R. K. Myers, and J. A. Fein. 2010. Using community-based participatory research to develop the PARTNERS youth violence prevention program. *Progress in Community Health Partnerships* 4(3):207–216. doi: 10.1353/cpr.2010.0005.

Limber, S. P., and M. A. Small. 2003. State laws and policies to address bullying in schools. *School Psychology Review* 32(3):445–455.

Limber, S. P., D. Olweus, and H. Luxenberg. 2013. *Bullying in U.S. schools: 2012 status report*. Center City, MN: Hazelden Foundation. http://www.violencepreventionworks.org/public/index.page (accessed May 19, 2014).

Lipsey, M. 2006. The effects of community-based group treatment for delinquency: A meta-analytic search for cross-study generalizations. In K. A. Dodge, T. J. Dishion, and J. E. Lansford (Eds.), *Deviant peer influences in programs for youth: Problems and solutions* (pp. 162–184). New York: Guilford.

Lochman, J., T. Dishion, C. Boxmeyer, and N. Powell. 2013. *Preliminary findings from NIDA-funded Study of Group versus Individual Intervention Format for the Coping Power Child Component*. Presented at the American Psychological Association meeting, Honolulu, Hawaii. July 31–August 4, 2013.

Lovegrove, P. J., A. D. Bellmore, J. Greif Green, K. Jens, and J. M. Ostrove. 2013. My voice is not going to be silent: What can parents do about children's bullying? *Journal of School Violence* 12(3):253–267. doi:10.1080/15388220.2013.792270.

Masten, C. L., N. I. Eisenberger, L. A. Borofsky, J. H. Pfeifer, K. McNealy, J. C. Mazziotta, and M. Dapretto. 2009. Neural correlates of social exclusion during adolescence: Understanding the distress of peer rejection. *Social Cognitive and Affective Neuroscience* 4(2):143–157.

Merrell, K., B. Gueldner, S. W. Ross, and D. Isava. 2008. How effective are school bullying intervention programs?: A meta-analysis of intervention research. *School Psychology Quarterly* 23(1):26–42.

Miller, S., J. Williams, S. Cutbush, D. Gibbs, M. Clinton-Sherrod, and S. Jones. 2013. Dating violence, bullying, and sexual harassment: Longitudinal profiles and transitions over time. *Journal of Youth Adolescence* 42(4):607–618.

Mitchell, K. J., M. L. Ybarra, and J. D. Korchmaros. 2013. Sexual harassment among adolescents of different sexual orientations and gender identities. *Child Abuse and Neglect* 38(2):280–295.

Modzeleski, W., T. Feucht, M. Rand, J. E. Hall, T. R. Simon, L. Butler, A. Taylor, M. Hunter, M. A. Anderson, L. Barrios, and M. Hertz. 2008. School-associated student homicides—United States, 1992–2006. *Morbidity and Mortality Weekly Report* 57(2):33–36. http://www.cdc.gov/mmwr/preview/mmwrhtml/mm5702a1.htm (accessed May 21, 2014).

Molcho, M., W. Craig, P. Due, W. Pickett, Y. Harel-Fisch, M. Overpeck, and the HBSC Bullying Writing Group. 2009. Cross-national time trends in bullying behaviour 1994–2006: Findings from Europe and North America. *International Journal of Public Health* 54:S225–S234.

Multisite Violence Prevention Project. 2009. The ecological effects of universal and selective violence prevention programs for middle school students: A randomized trial. *Journal of Consulting and Clinical Psychology* 77(3):526–542.

Musher-Eizenman, D. R., P. Boxer, S. Danner, E. F. Dubow, S. E. Goldstein, and D. M. I. Heretick. 2004. Social-cognitive mediators of the relation of environmental and emotion regulation factors to children's aggression. *Aggressive Behavior* 30:389–408.

NRC (National Research Council) and IOM (Institute of Medicine). 2009. *Preventing mental, emotional, and behavioral disorders among young people: Progress and possibilities.* Washington, DC: The National Academies Press.

O'Connell, P., D. Pepler, and W. Craig. 1999. Peer involvement in bullying: Insights and challenges for intervention. *Journal of Adolescence* 22:437–452.

Odgers, C. L., T. E. Moffitt, L. M. Tach, R. J. Sampson, A. Taylor, C. L. Matthews, and A. Caspi. 2009. The protective effects of neighborhood collective efficacy on British children growing up in deprivation: A developmental analysis. *Developmental Psychology* 45(4):942–957. doi:10.1037/a0016162.

Olweus, D. 1991. Bully/victim problems among schoolchildren: Basic facts and effects of a school based intervention program. In D. J. Pepler and H. Rubin (Eds.), *The development and treatment of childhood aggression* (pp. 411–448). Hillsdale, NJ: Erlbaum.

Olweus, D. 1993. *Bullying at school: What we know and what we can do.* Malden, MA: Blackwell Publishing Ltd.

Olweus, D. 1997. Bully/victim problems in school: Facts and intervention. *European Journal of Psychology of Education* 12:495–510.

Olweus, D. 2012. School bullying: Development and some important challenges. *Annual Review of Clinical Psychology* 9:751–780.

Olweus, D., S. P. Limber, V. Flerx, N. Mullin, J. Riese, and M. Snyder. 2007. *Olweus Bullying Prevention Program: Schoolwide guide.* Center City, MN: Hazelden.

Ouellet-Morin, I., A. Danese, L. Bowes, S. Shakoor, A. Ambler, C. M. Pariante, A. S. Papadopoulos, A. Caspi, T. E. Moffitt, and L. Arseneault. 2011. A discordant monozygotic twin design shows blunted cortisol reactivity among bullied children. *Journal of American Academy of Child and Adolescent Psychiatry* 50(6):574–582.

Payne, A. A., D. C. Gottfredson, and G. D. Gottfredson. 2003. Schools as communities: The relationships among communal school organization, student bonding, and school disorder. *Criminology* 41:749–777.

Polanin, J. R., D. L. Espelage, and T. D. Pigott. 2012. A meta-analysis of school-based bullying prevention programs' effects on bystander intervention behavior. *School Psychology Review* 41:47–65.

Rao, M. A., D. L. Espelage, and T. D. Little. In press. Links between family conflict and substance-use in early adolescence: The mediating role of peer victimization. *Developmental Psychology.*

Reijntjes, A., J. H. Kamphuis, P. Prinzie, and M. Telch. 2010. Peer victimization and internalizing problems in children: A meta-analysis of longitudinal studies. *Child Abuse & Neglect* 34:244–252.

Rigby, K., and P. T. Slee. 1993. Dimensions of interpersonal relation among Australian children and implications for psychological well-being. *British Journal of Educational Psychology* 133:33–42.

Ringwalt, C. L., A. A. Vincus, S. T. Ennett, S. Hanley, J. M. Bowling, and L. A. Rohrbach. 2009. The prevalence of evidence-based substance use prevention curricula in U.S. middle schools in 2005. *Prevention Science* 10:33–40.

Rivers, I., and N. Noret. 2013. Potential suicide ideation and its association with observing bullying at school. *Journal of Adolescent Health* 53:S32–S36.

Robers, S., J. Zhang, J. Truman, and T. D. Snyder. 2010. *Indicators of school crime and safety: 2010*. (NCES 1001-002/NCJ 230812.) Washington, DC: National Center for Education Statistics, U.S. Department of Education, and Bureau of Justice Statistics, Office of Justice Programs, U.S. Department of Justice.

Robers, S., J. Zhang, J. Truman, and T. D. Snyder. 2012. *Indicators of school crime and safety: 2011*. (NCES 2012-002/NCJ 236021). Washington, DC: National Center for Education Statistics, U.S. Department of Education, and Bureau of Justice Statistics, Office of Justice Programs, U.S. Department of Justice.

Robers, S., J. Kemp, J. Truman, and T. D. Snyder. 2013. *Indicators of school crime and safety: 2012*. (NCES 2013-036/NCJ 241446). Washington, DC: National Center for Education Statistics, U.S. Department of Education, and Bureau of Justice Statistics, Office of Justice Programs, U.S. Department of Justice.

Rohrbach, L. A., and S. Dyal. In press. Scaling up prevention programs in schools. In K. Bosworth (Ed.), *Prevention science in school settings: Complex relationships and processes*. New York: Springer Publishers.

Rohrbach, L. A., J. W. Graham, and W. B. Hansen. 1993. Diffusion of a school-based substance abuse prevention program: Predictors of program implementation. *Preventive Medicine* 22(2):237–260.

Rohrbach, L. A., R. Grana, T. W. Valente, and S. Sussman. 2006. Type II translation: Transporting prevention interventions from research to real-world settings. *Evaluation and the Health Professions* 29(3):302–333.

Salmivalli, C., A. Kärnä, and E. Poskiparta. 2011. Counteracting bullying in Finland: The KiVa program and its effects on different forms of being bullied. *International Journal of Behavioral Development* 35(5):405–411.

Saul, J., A. Wandersman, P. Flaspohler, J. Duffy, K. Lubell, and R. Noonan. 2008. Research and action for bridging the gap between prevention research and practice. *American Journal of Community Psychology* 41:3–4.

Schacter H. L., S. J. White, V. Y. Chang, and J. Juvonen. 2014. "Why me?": Characterological self-blame and continued victimization in the first year of middle school. *Journal of Clinical Child and Adolescent Psychology* 43(3):1–10.

Shalev, I., T. E. Moffitt, K. Sugden, B. Williams, R. M. Houts, A. Danese, J. Mill, L. Arseneault, and A. Caspi. 2013. Exposure to violence during childhood is associated with telomere erosion from 5 to 10 years of age: A longitudinal study. *Molecular Psychiatry* 18(5):576–581.

Smith, E. P., D. Gorman-Smith, W. H. Quinn, D. L. Rabiner, P. H. Tolan, and D. M. Winn. 2004. Community-based multiple family groups to prevent and reduce violent and aggressive behavior: The GREAT Families Program. *American Journal of Preventive Medicine* 26(1):39–47.

Smokowski, P. R., and K. H. Kopasz. 2005. Bullying in school: An overview of types, effects, family characteristics, and intervention strategies. *Children & Schools* 27(2):101–110.

Snyder, H. N., and M. Sickmund. 2006. *Juvenile offenders and victims: 2006 national report*. Washington, DC: U.S. Department of Justice, Office of Justice Programs, Office of Juvenile Justice and Delinquency Prevention. http://www.ojjdp.gov/ojstatbb/nr2006/downloads/NR2006.pdf (accessed May 22, 2014).

Sourander, A., J. A. Rönning, H. Eloheimo, S. Nimelä, H. Helenius, K. Kumpulainen, J. Piha, T. Tamminen, I. Moilanen, and F. Almqvist. 2007. Childhood bullies and victims and their risk of criminality in late adolescence: The Finnish from a Boy to a Man Study. *Archives of Pediatric Adolescent Medicine* 161(6):546–552.

Spoth, R., L. A. Rohrbach, M. Greenberg, P. Leaf, C. Brown, A. Fagan, R. Catalano, M. Pentz, Z. Sloboda, and J. Hawkins. 2013. Addressing core challenges for the next generation of Type 2 translation research and systems: The Translation Science to Population Impact (TSci Impact) framework. *Prevention Science* 14(4):319–351.

Srabstein, J. C., B. E. Berkman, and E. Pyntikova. 2008. Antibullying legislation: A public health perspective. *Journal of Adolescent Health* 42:11–20.

Swearer, S. M., J. Peugh, D. L. Espelage, A. B. Siebecker, W. L. Kingsbury, and K. S. Bevins. 2006. A socioecological model for bullying prevention and intervention in early adolescence: An exploratory examination. In S. R. Jimerson and M. Furlong (Eds.), *Handbook of school violence and school safety: From research to practice* (pp. 257–273). Mahwah, NJ: Erlbaum.

Tierney, J. P., J. B. Grossman, and N. L. Resch. 1995. *Making a difference: An impact study of Big Brothers Big Sisters*. Philadelphia, PA: Public/Private Ventures.

Tolan, P. H., D. Gorman-Smith, D. B. Henry, and M. Schoeny. 2010. The effects of a booster prevention program on child behavior and family functioning: The SAFE Children program. *Prevention Science* 10:287–297.

Ttofi, M. M., and D. P. Farrington. 2011. Effectiveness of school-based programs to reduce bullying: A systematic and meta-analytic review. *Journal of Experimental Criminology* 7(1):27–56.

Ttofi, M. M., D. P. Farrington, F. Lösel, and R. Loeber. 2011a. Do the victims of school bullies tend to become depressed later in life? A systematic review and meta-analysis of longitudinal studies. *Journal of Aggression, Conflict and Peace Research* 3:63–73.

Ttofi, M. M., D. P. Farrington, F. Lösel, and R. Loeber. 2011b. The predictive efficiency of school bullying versus later offending: A systematic/meta-analytic review of longitudinal studies. *Criminal Behavior and Mental Health* 21(2):80–89.

Unnever, J. D., and D. G. Cornell. 2003. The culture of bullying in middle school. *Journal of School Violence* 2:5–27.

U.S. Department of Education. 2010. Dear colleague letter. http://www2.ed.gov/about/offices/list/ocr/letters/colleague-201010.html (accessed May 19, 2014).

U.S. Department of Education. 2011. *Analysis of state bullying laws and policies*. Washington, DC: U.S. Department of Education, Office of Planning, Evaluation and Policy Development, Policy and Program Studies Service.

U. S. Department of Education. 2013. Dear Colleague Letter. http://www.ed.gov/blog/2013/08/keeping-students-with-disabilities-safe-from-bullying (accessed June 19, 2014).

U.S. Secret Service and U.S. Department of Education. 2002. *The final report and findings of the Safe School Initiative: Implications for the prevention of school attacks in the United States*. Washington, DC: U.S. Department of Education.

Vaillancourt, T., E. Duku, S. Becker, L. A. Schmidt, J. Nicol, C. Muir, and H. Macmillan. 2011. Peer victimization, depressive symptoms, and high salivary cortisol predict poorer memory in children. *Brain and Cognition* 77(2):191–199.

Voisin, D. R., and J. S. Hong. 2012. A conceptual formulation examining the relationship between witnessing domestic violence and bullying behaviors and victimization among youth. *Educational Psychology Review* 24(4):479–498.

Waasdorp, T. E., C. P. Bradshaw, and P. J. Leaf. 2012. The impact of School-Wide Positive Behavioral Interventions and Supports (SWPBIS) on bullying and peer rejection: A randomized controlled effectiveness trial. *Archives of Pediatrics and Adolescent Medicine* 116(2):149–156.

Woolf, S. H. 2008. The meaning of translational research and why it matters. *JAMA* 299(2): 211–213.

Wright, J., R. Sege, and the American Academy of Pediatrics Committee on Injury Violence and Poison Prevention. 2009. Role of the pediatrician in youth violence prevention. *Pediatrics* 124(1):393–402, doi: 10.1542/peds.2009-0943.

Ybarra, M. L., A. T. Bağci Bosi, J. Korchmaros, and S. Emri. 2012. A text messaging-based smoking cessation program for adult smokers: randomized controlled trial. *Journal of Medical Internet Research* 14(6):e172.

Ybarra, M. L., S. S. Bull, T. L. Prescott, J. D. Korchmaros, D. R. Bangsberg, and J. P. Kiwanuka. 2013a. Adolescent abstinence and unprotected sex in CyberSenga, an Internet-based HIV prevention program: Randomized clinical trial of efficacy. *PLoS ONE* 8(8):e70083.

Ybarra, M. L., J. S. Holtrop, T. L. Prescott, M. H. Rahbar, and D. Strong. 2013b. Pilot RCT results of stop my smoking USA: A text messaging–based smoking cessation program for young adults. *Nicotine and Tobacco Research* 15(8):1388–1399.

Yeager, D. S., C. J. Fong, H. Y. Lee, and D. L. Espelage. In press. Declines in efficacy of anti-bullying programs among older adolescents: A developmental theory and a three-level meta-analysis. *Journal of Applied Developmental Psychology.*

Zimmerman, F. J., G. M. Glew, D. A. Christakis, and W. Katon. 2005. Early cognitive stimulation, emotional support, and television watching as predictors of subsequent bullying among grade-school children. *Archive of Pediatrics and Adolescent Medicine* 159(4):384–388.

# B

# Workshop Agenda

BUILDING CAPACITY TO REDUCE BULLYING AND ITS IMPACT ON YOUTH ACROSS THE LIFECOURSE: A WORKSHOP

April 9–10, 2014

National Academy of Sciences Building
2101 Constitution Ave., NW, Washington, DC
Lecture Room

AGENDA

*Workshop Goals and Objectives*

The overall objective of the workshop is to highlight current research on bullying prevention. More specifically, workshop presentations and discussions will address the following questions:

- What is the underlying knowledge base and conceptual models that guide the design, delivery, and evaluation of bullying prevention and intervention efforts?
- Are there specific interventions that are effective in decreasing bullying and the antecedents to bullying?
- What programs designed to address other negative adolescent behaviors (e.g., substance abuse, delinquency, etc.) are also effective at preventing or reducing bullying?
- Are there specific models and interventions that increase protective factors and mitigate the negative health impact of bullying?
- What are the key sectors involved in bullying prevention and intervention? How does involvement or lack of involvement by key sectors influence opportunities and barriers to implementing a

blueprint for bullying prevention and intervention? What are some appropriate roles for each of the key sectors in preventing bullying?

DAY 1: April 9, 2014

| | |
|---|---|
| 8:30–8:45 a.m. | **Welcome and Overview of Agenda**<br>Frederick P. Rivara (Planning Committee Chair), University of Washington School of Medicine |
| 8:45–9:00 a.m. | **Perspectives from the Sponsor**<br>Michael C. Lu, Health Resources and Services Administration |
| 9:00–9:30 a.m. | **Introduction and Role of Youth Panelists**<br>Moderator: Megan Moreno, University of Washington<br><br>Alexa Cafasso, Student at Sacred Heart Academy<br>Glenn Cantave, Student at Wesleyan University<br>Whitney Dockrey, Student at Georgetown University<br>Asher Farkas, Student at New York University<br>Rebecca Shaw, Student at Horace Mann School |
| 9:30–9:50 a.m. | **Introduction and Role of School Personnel Panelists**<br>Moderator: Catherine Bradshaw, University of Virginia and Planning Committee<br><br>Virginia L. Dolan, Anne Arundel County Public Schools<br>Mike Donlin, State of Washington Office of Superintendent of Public Instruction<br>William Myers, South River High School |
| 9:50–10:20 a.m. | **Overview of Bullying and Victimization**<br>Session Objectives:<br>• Provide an overview of key issues relevant to bullying and victimization (including Centers for Disease Control and Prevention definition, frequency, and consequences [immediate, long-term effects on health, school, quality of life]). Discuss types of bullying (physical, verbal, relational, damage to property, and cyber). |

- Discuss roles in bullying (bully, victim, bully–victim, bystander).

*Susan Limber, Clemson University*

| | |
|---|---|
| 10:20–11:20 a.m. | **Session 1: Targets of Bullying and Bullying Behavior**<br>Session Objective:<br>• Highlight current research on risk factors, protective factors, and resiliency associated with targets of bullying and bullying behavior at the individual, family, school, and community levels.<br>Moderator: *Catherine Bradshaw, University of Virginia*<br><br>*Jaana Juvonen, University of California, Los Angeles*<br>*Tracy Vaillancourt, University of Ottawa*<br>*Dorothy Espelage, University of Illinois, Urbana-Champaign*<br>*Robert Faris, University of California, Davis* |
| 11:20–11:50 a.m. | **Discussion and Audience Q & A**<br>Discussant: *Catherine Bradshaw* |
| 11:50 a.m.–12:50 p.m. | **Lunch** |
| 12:50–1:35 p.m. | **Session 2: School-Based Interventions**<br>Session Objective:<br>• Highlight current research on school-based interventions including school policies, school climate, and preventive interventions.<br>Moderator: *Nina Fredland, Texas Woman's University College of Nursing*<br><br>*Denise Gottfredson, University of Maryland*<br>*Catherine Bradshaw, University of Virginia*<br>*Dewey Cornell, University of Virginia* |
| 1:35–2:05 p.m. | **Discussion and Audience Q & A**<br>Discussant: *Nina Fredland* |

| | |
|---|---|
| 2:05–2:50 p.m. | **Session 3: Family-Focused Interventions**<br>Session Objective:<br>• Highlight current research on family-level interventions including parenting, responses to bullying behavior, and parental awareness of kids' online presence.<br>Moderator: *Jonathan Todres, Georgia State University College of Law*<br><br>*Melissa Holt, Boston University*<br>*Deborah Gorman-Smith, University of Chicago* |
| 2:50–3:20 p.m. | **Discussion and Audience Q & A**<br>Discussant: *Jonathan Todres* |
| 3:20–3:35 p.m. | **Break** |
| 3:35–4:05 p.m. | **Session 4: Technology-Based Interventions**<br>Session Objective:<br>• Highlight current research on technology-based interventions, including social media–based campaigns and using technology to disseminate interventions.<br>Moderator: *Megan Moreno, University of Washington*<br><br>*Michele Ybarra, Center for Innovative Public Health Research*<br>*Faye Mishna, University of Toronto* |
| 4:05–4:35 p.m. | **Discussion and Audience Q & A**<br>Discussant: *Megan Moreno* |
| 4:35 p.m. | **Adjourn Day 1** |

DAY 2: April 10, 2014

| | |
|---|---|
| 8:30–8:40 a.m. | **Welcome and Overview of Agenda**<br>*Frederick P. Rivara, Planning Committee Chair* |

| | |
|---|---|
| 8:40–9:10 a.m. | **Session 5: Community-Based Interventions**<br>Session Objective:<br>• Highlight current research on community-based interventions including the role of health care providers.<br>Moderator: *Angela Diaz, Mount Sinai Hospital and Chair, Board on Children, Youth, and Families*<br><br>*Asha Goldweber, SRI International*<br>*Joseph L. Wright, George Washington University Schools of Medicine and Public Health* |
| 9:10–9:40 a.m. | **Discussion and Audience Q & A**<br>Discussant: *Angela Diaz* |
| 9:40–10:10 a.m. | **Session 6: Peer-Led and Peer-Focused Programs**<br>Session Objective:<br>• Highlight current research on peer-led programs related to bullying prevention and related areas of research.<br>Moderator: *Jonathan Todres, Georgia State University College of Law*<br><br>*Tom Dishion, Arizona State University*<br>*Kenneth A. Dodge, Duke University* |
| 10:10–10:40 a.m. | **Discussion and Audience Q & A**<br>Discussant: *Jonathan Todres* |
| 10:40–11:00 a.m. | **Break** |
| 11:00–11:30 a.m. | **Session 7: Laws and Public Policies**<br>Session Objectives:<br>• Provide an overview of anti-bullying laws and policies.<br>• Discuss opportunities provided by legal framework, constraints, and challenges.<br>Moderator: *Jonathan Todres, Georgia State University College of Law*<br><br>*Mark Hatzenbuehler, Columbia University*<br>*Douglas E. Abrams, University of Missouri School of Law* |

| | |
|---|---|
| 11:30 a.m.–12:00 p.m. | **Discussion and Audience Q & A**<br>Discussant: *Jonathan Todres* |
| 12:00–1:00 p.m. | **Lunch** |
| 1:00–1:45 p.m. | **Session 8: Translating Bullying Research into Policy and Practice**<br>Session Objective:<br>• Highlight the current research on the science of implementation, increasing capacity, and sustainability, including implementing community-wide systems interventions.<br>Moderator: *Denise Gottfredson, University of Maryland*<br><br>*Abigail Fagan, University of Florida*<br>*Luanne Rohrbach, University of Southern California*<br>*C. Hendricks Brown, Northwestern University* |
| 1:45–2:15 p.m. | **Discussion and Audience Q & A**<br>Discussant: *Denise Gottfredson* |
| 2:15–2:45 p.m. | **School Personnel Reaction Panel**<br>Session Objectives: Comment on the workshop presentations and discussions, including<br>• What seemed particularly important and/or useful?<br>• What important issues were missing from the workshop discussion?<br>Moderator: *Catherine Bradshaw, University of Virginia*<br><br>*Virginia L. Dolan, Mike Donlin, and William Myers* |
| 2:45–3:30 p.m. | **Youth Reaction Panel**<br>Session Objectives: Comment on the workshop presentations and discussions, including<br>• What seemed particularly important and/or useful? |

|  |  |
|---|---|
|  | • What important issues were missing from the workshop discussion?<br>Moderator: *Megan Moreno, University of Washington*<br><br>*Alexa Cafasso, Glenn Cavante, Whitney Dockrey, Asher Farkas, and Rebecca Shaw* |
| 3:30–4:30 p.m. | **Future Directions and Next Steps**<br>Session Objectives:<br>• Synthesize and discuss key highlights from the workshop presentations and discussions.<br>• Identify key promising areas for future research and policy, key challenges, key opportunities.<br>Moderator: *Frederick P. Rivara, Planning Committee Chair*<br><br>*Catherine Bradshaw, Nina Fredland, Denise Gottfredson, Megan Moreno, and Jonathan Todres* |
| 4:30 p.m. | **Adjourn** |

# C

# Workshop Statement of Task

An ad hoc planning committee will plan and conduct a 2-day public workshop that highlights relevant information and knowledge that can inform a multi-disciplinary road map on next steps for the field of bullying prevention. Content areas that will be explored include the identification of conceptual models and interventions that have proven effective in decreasing bullying and the antecedents to bullying, while increasing protective factors that mitigate the negative health impact of bullying. Key sectors that are involved in bullying prevention will be identified in order to understand the opportunities and barriers to implementing a blueprint for bullying prevention. An individually authored workshop summary will be prepared based on the information gathered and the discussions held during the workshop session. The workshop will feature invited presentations and discussions that address the following questions:

- What is the underlying knowledge base and conceptual models that guide the design, delivery, and evaluation of bullying prevention and intervention efforts?
- Are there specific interventions that are effective in decreasing bullying and the antecedents to bullying?
- What programs designed to address other negative adolescent behaviors (e.g., substance abuse, delinquency, etc.) are also effective at preventing or reducing bullying?
- Are there specific models and interventions that increase protective factors and mitigate negative health impact of bullying?

- What are the key sectors involved in bullying prevention and intervention? How does involvement or lack of involvement by key sectors influence opportunities and barriers to implementing a blueprint for bullying prevention and intervention? What are some appropriate roles for each of the key sectors in preventing bullying?

This activity constitutes Phase 1 of a three-part effort directed toward examining, analyzing, and synthesizing information and knowledge about policy, education, and behavioral strategies aimed at decreasing bullying behavior.